Coaching for Performance

The business agenda at the start of the twenty-first century focuses on working with change and developing people's potential and performance. The *People Skills for Professionals* series brings this leading theme to life with a practical range of personal development and human resource guides for anyone who wants to get the best from their people.

Other titles in the Series

COACHING CLUES
Real stories, Powerful Solutions
Practical Tools
Marian J. Thier

LEADING YOUR TEAM
How to Involve and Inspire Teams
Second edition
Andrew Leigh and Michael Maynard

MANAGING TRANSITIONS
Making the Most of Change
Second edition
William Bridges

MEDIATION FOR MANAGERS
Resolving Conflict and
Rebuilding Relationships at Work
John Crawley and Katherine Graham

THE NEW NEGOTIATING EDGE
The Behavioral Approach for
Results and Relationships
Gavin Kennedy

NLP AT WORK
The Difference that Makes the
Difference in Business
Second edition
Sue Knight

Coaching for Performance

GROWing People, Performance and Purpose

Third edition

John Whitmore

NICHOLAS BREALEY
PUBLISHING
LONDON

This third edition first published by
Nicholas Brealey Publishing in 2002
Reprinted 2002, 2003, 2004, 2005, 2006, 2007 (twice)

First published in 1992

3–5 Spafield Street
Clerkenwell, London
EC1R 4QB, UK
Tel: +44 (0)20 7239 0360
Fax: +44 (0)20 7239 0370

20 Park Plaza, Suite 1115A
Boston
MA 02116, USA
Tel: (888) BREALEY
Fax: (617) 523 3708

www.nicholasbrealey.com
www.performanceconsultants.com

© John Whitmore 1992, 1996, 2002
The right of John Whitmore to be identified as the author of this work has been asserted in accordance with the Copyright, Designs and Patents Act 1988.

ISBN-10: 1-85788-303-9
ISBN-13: 978-1-85788-303-9

British Library Cataloguing in Publication Data
A catalogue record for this book is available from the British Library.

Printed in Finland by WS Bookwell.

Contents

Acknowledgments   vii

Introduction   1

1   What Is Coaching?   7

2   The Manager as Coach   20

3   The Nature of Change   26

4   The Nature of Coaching   32

5   Effective Questions   44

6   The Sequence of Questioning   53

7   Goal Setting   57

8   What Is Reality?   67

9   What Options Do You Have?   81

10   What Will You Do?   88

11   What Is Performance?   97

12   Learning and Enjoyment   102

13   Motivation   108

14   Coaching for Purpose   115

15   Coaching for Meaning   119

16   Coaching the Corporation   127

17   Feedback and Assessment   134

18   The Development of a Team   145

19   Coaching Teams   152

20   Overcoming Barriers to Coaching   158

21   The Multiple Benefits of Coaching   166

22   Conclusion   170

Appendix   173

Bibliography   179

Acknowledgments

Any book of this nature will be the product of the author's exposure to and learning from many experiences and many people.

Tim Gallwey must undoubtedly head the list, as the creator of the Inner Game, followed in chronological order by Bob Kriegel, Sarah Ferguson, Graham Alexander, Alan Fine, Caroline Harris, Chris Morgan, Miles Downey and Peter Lightfoot, who all started as Inner Game sports coaches and who have since applied their coaching skills in business with great effect. I would recommend each of them as excellent coaches, along with Drs Alan Beggs and Lew Hardy who also provided academic respectability to Inner Game ideas, which encouraged us when rejection by traditionalists was widely available.

I am especially grateful to my two longstanding coaching colleagues, David Hemery and David Whitaker, with whom I have taught countless courses and shared creative ideas. Both were successful performers and coaches who reached Olympian heights, and who also reached similar conclusions to the rest of us through their own experiences. This third edition is a product of recent years of training and coaching experience with my band of colleagues at Performance Consultants, and our many clients. I thank you all.

My wife Diana runs an educational charity that trains psychotherapists and counselors. She has monitored the development of my people skills over the years, keeping me in line with conventional wisdom and guiding me through the minefield of the deeper aspects of the human psyche. My son Jason, a junior county champion tennis player and talented skier, has co-authored with me a tennis book for children. From him I have learned much too.

Finally, thanks to Nick Brealey, who has given me feedback, encouragement, criticism and suggestions that have made this a far better book than it might otherwise have been.

For information about Performance Consultants International
and the Performance Coach Training, Performance Coaching,
Leadership and Team Development programs and services
provided by John Whitmore and his associates
please contact:

David Brown, Chief Executive Officer

Performance Consultants International

Direct: +44 (0)792 1360 343

Office: +44 (0)207 3736 431

Email: davidbrown@performanceconsultants.com

Website: www.performanceconsultants.com

Introduction

Coaching has been a buzzword in business circles for some time now. Attend any gathering of executives, personnel directors, human resource experts, entrepreneurs or trainers and you cannot fail to hear the word coaching spoken as frequently as profit or recession.

It is 20 years since I first applied coaching in a business context and 10 years since I wrote the first edition of this book. It has become widely accepted as the definitive book on coaching methodology in the business context. The fact that it is now published in a dozen languages, including Japanese, Russian and Malaysian, indicates that coaching has gone global.

Unfortunately, the popularizing of the term led both the well-meaning and the unscrupulous to apply it to their old wares. Consequently coaching has been in danger of being misrepresented, misperceived and dismissed as not so new and different and as failing to live up to its promises. Furthermore, many business autocrats genuinely believe that they are positively democratic and that they use coaching as a matter of course. Since such people have no equals to give them feedback to the contrary, and their subordinates would never dare to enlighten them, in ignorance they continue to demean both their workforce and the currency of coaching.

THE SKILL, ART AND PRACTICE OF COACHING

Coaching is a management behavior that lies at the opposite end of the spectrum to command and control

The purpose of this book is to keep the record straight by describing and illustrating what coaching really is, what it can be used for, when and how much it can be used, who can use it well and who cannot. Contrary to the attractive claims of the *One Minute Manager*, there are no quick fixes in business, and good coaching is a skill, an art perhaps, that requires a depth of understanding and plenty of practice if it is to deliver its astonishing potential. Reading this book will not turn you into an expert coach, but it will help you to recognize the enormous value and potential of coaching, and perhaps set you on a journey of self-discovery that will have a profound effect on your business success, your sporting and other skills, and the quality of how you relate to others at work and at home.

This remains as true today as it did when the first edition of this book was published in 1992. The good news is that coaching did not turn out to be merely the flavor of the month, or even of the year, as some cynics had predicted. Coaching has now achieved widespread recognition as being of value, relevance and importance in business. It is championed by the great and good of the business community.

The bad news is that the hunger for coaching has resulted in hastily and inadequately trained managers, or so-called coaches, failing to meet the expectations of those they are coaching. In too many cases they have not fully understood the performance-related, psychological principles on which coaching is based. Without this understanding they may go through the motions of coaching, or use the behaviors associated with coaching, such as questioning, but fail to achieve the intended results.

I hasten to reassure the potential coach, however, that the beauty of coaching lies in its depth and impact, and that you don't need a degree in psychology in order to practice it. This third edition explains more fully the principles of coaching in lay terms and illustrates them with simple analogies, not only from business but also from sport. Deeper principles are often more easily grasped away from the biases and assumptions of one's own field of application.

This edition clarifies still further the process and practice of coaching by drawing on the experience gained from the thousands of hours of training that my colleagues and I have delivered to many thousands of participants in the intervening ten years.

It has another purpose also. Over the years, several books on coaching have appeared, some focusing exclusively on the application of coaching to personal or career development. While this is a hugely productive field, it is not, in my opinion, the most important application of the coaching principles; but more about that later.

Other books and articles have focused on the coach as the detached outsider. Directors of large corporations, and chief executives in particular, may be gregarious, but they can also be very lonely. There are not many people to whom they can turn for help, often no one in their own organization. Uncertainty about trust and confidentiality, covert in-house competition and the slipperiness of the corporate ladder often make it hard for a CEO to turn to a boardroom colleague about issues that may concern their own or a peer's performance or tenure. Perhaps even more common, however, is simply the wish to consult a fresh mind, someone who brings no investment or position of his own, an outsider who is not involved with the organization or its culture. An independent coach can reflect ideas, evoke solutions and support their implementation in a way that few insiders could ever do.

Senior executives are increasingly recognizing the benefits and opportunities of exploring new avenues in consultations with a coach scheduled on a regular basis. The same is true for senior business teams, who may spend most of their time scattered far and wide. When they do get

EXECUTIVE COACHING

A skillful coach rarely provides or prescribes solutions

together, they want their meetings to be as productive as possible, and team facilitation by an independent coach is an excellent way to achieve that. The coach is able to monitor the dynamics of the team and attend to group process while assisting and freeing the team to focus on the task. The demand for good independent coaches is growing in all areas.

LIFE BALANCE

In our coaching courses for managers we often include a segment on 'life balance'. We have managers coach each other to increase their awareness of the balance, or lack of it, in their lives between work and a number of factors such as their partner, children, leisure, adventure, quiet time for the soul, health and fitness, contribution and community.

Business has taken over too much of too many people's lives at too high a personal cost. Too many executives and managers live to work rather than work to live. Stress, broken marriages, neglected children and poor health are far more widespread than most business people dare to acknowledge. Coaching is a gentle way of raising awareness of the imbalances that exist, and of helping the coachee to find a way forward that will benefit their work and their play. This will often involve creating a vision of the future or an ideal to aspire toward, as opposed to struggling to survive by avoiding problems.

Many executives are finding that regular coaching sessions with an external coach, even by telephone when necessary, can have a transformational impact on the quality of their performance at work and their relationships at home. While this is an immensely valuable proactive application of coaching, it is in one sense curative rather than preventive. If the predominant management ethos of a company is coaching, the vital factor of balance is simply part of the agenda for good management and performance, and the problems rarely arise in the first place.

SELF-COACHING

One more useful, but still not the most useful, application of coaching that is often bypassed by trainers and seldom referred to in the literature is self-coaching. Anyone who truly understands coaching will soon begin to coach themselves on everything from career choices to their golf swing, including those very personal issues that they would be most reluctant to share with another. After all, self-coaching is a safe way to practice and develop the skill of coaching, which can then be applied to others with confidence.

So what *is* the most important application of coaching? Only when coaching principles govern or underlie all management behavior and interactions, as they certainly will do in time, will the full force of people's performance potential be released. This third edition of *Coaching for Performance* is a further call for the wide recognition and employment of these fundamental performance principles throughout the work place and work time. Although it may contradict some conventional beliefs about performance and challenge some habits of a lifetime, its common sense will be hard to deny or reject. It is a call for us to come to our senses, both literally and metaphorically. **It is a call for a fundamental transformation of management style and culture.** The inability of so many businesses to move beyond the language of culture change to its practice remains a major block.

In this new edition I have added a section (Chapters 14–16) dealing with the recently recognized significance to performance of emotional intelligence (EQ), the emerging interest in spiritual intelligence (SQ) and how they both relate to coaching. Higher workplace expectations of staff and the frequency with which they seek meaning and purpose at work mean that coaches will be expected to acquire greater skill in addressing these deeper life issues. We will look at what those skills are and how they can be developed. Companies are also having to accept that their values and ethics are falling and in some cases failing under the scrutiny of their staff as well as their customers. Coaching is highly effective for uncovering true values and producing the alignment without which business performance can never be optimized.

A CULTURE OF COACHING

MEANING AND PURPOSE

GENDER

Throughout this book I will more often use the masculine gender, not because I am sexist, which I am not, nor because I abhor the literary clumsiness of 'he or she' and 'his or her', which I do, but because it is men who need to heed its message most. On the coaching courses my colleagues and I run, women have consistently shown more natural ability to adopt a coaching philosophy. It is more in line with their style. Perhaps the advent of more and more women into senior managerial roles will help to establish the practice of coaching as the communication norm throughout business. I hope so, and I hope that some of them will find the coaching model in this book useful.

EXAMPLES

Problems must be resolved at the level beneath the one at which they occur

I will use examples and analogies from business and from a variety of sports to illustrate particular points and, to clarify the process further, I provide the dialog of an imaginary but typical coaching session. There is also a table of standard questions, which could form the basis of a coaching session, questions on which the coach would obviously build and elaborate according to the particular circumstances.

Although I advocate coaching as a management style rather than merely a tool for a manager or consultant to use occasionally, much of this book is devoted to conveying a deeper understanding of coaching principles by breaking its elements down and giving examples from structured coaching sessions. Full integration into management style will only come with time and practice.

1
What Is Coaching?

Coaching focuses on future possibilities, not past mistakes.

The *Concise Oxford Dictionary* defines the verb to coach as to 'tutor, train, give hints to, prime with facts'. This does not help us much, for those things can be done in many ways, some of which bear no relationship to coaching. Coaching is as much about the way these things are done as about what is done. Coaching delivers results in large measure because of the supportive relationship between the coach and the coachee, and the means and style of communication used. The coachee does acquire the facts, not from the coach but from within himself, stimulated by the coach. Of course, the objective of improving performance is paramount, but how that is best achieved is what is in question.

THE SPORTING ORIGINS OF COACHING

For some reason we have tennis coaches but ski instructors. Both for the most part, in my experience, are instructors. In recent years tennis instruction has become somewhat less dogmatic and technique based, but still has a very long way to go. Ski instruction in Britain has moved a long way from where it was toward coaching, but European ski instruction is still of the 'Bend zee knees' variety and lags behind the United States.

THE INNER GAME

A coach recognizes that the internal obstacles are often more daunting than the external ones

The teaching of both these sports, and also golf, was tackled over two decades ago by Harvard educationalist and tennis expert Timothy Gallwey, who threw down the gauntlet with a book entitled *The Inner Game of Tennis*, quickly followed by *Inner Skiing* and *The Inner Game of Golf*. The word 'inner' was used to indicate the player's internal state or, to use Gallwey's words, 'the opponent within one's own head is more formidable than the one the other side of the net'. Anyone who has had one of those days on the court when he couldn't do anything right will recognize what Gallwey is referring to. Gallwey went on to claim that if a coach can help a player to remove or reduce the internal obstacles to their performance, an unexpected natural ability will flow forth without the need for much technical input from the coach.

At the time his books first appeared, few coaches, instructors or pros could believe, let alone embrace, his ideas, although players devoured them eagerly in best-seller-list quantities. The professionals' ground of being was under threat. They thought that Gallwey was trying to turn the teaching of sport on its head and that he was undermining their egos, their authority and the principles in which they had invested so much. In a way he was, but their fear exaggerated their fantasies about his intentions. He was not threatening them with redundancy, but merely proposing that they would be more effective if they changed their approach.

THE ESSENCE OF COACHING

And Gallwey **had** put his finger on the essence of coaching. **Coaching is unlocking a person's potential to maximize their own performance. It is helping them to learn rather than teaching them**.

This was not new: Socrates had voiced the same things some 2000 years earlier, but somehow his philosophy was lost in the rush to materialistic reductionism of the last two centuries. The pendulum has swung back and coaching, if not Socrates, is here to stay for a generation or two! Gallwey's books coincided with the emergence in psychological understanding of a more optimistic model of humankind than the old behaviorist view that we are little more than empty vessels into which everything has to be poured. The new model suggested we are more like an acorn, which contains within it all the potential to be a magnificent oak tree. We need nourishment, encouragement and the light to reach toward, but the oaktreeness is already within.

It may be harder to give up instructing than it is to learn to coach

If we accept this model, and it is only contested by some aging flat earthers, the way we learn, and more importantly the way we teach and instruct, must be called into question. Unfortunately, habits die hard and old methods persist even though most of us know their limitations.

Let me extend the acorn analogy a step further. You may not be aware that oak saplings, growing from acorns in the wild, quickly develop a single, hair-thin tap root to seek out water. This may extend downwards as far as a meter while the sapling is still only 30 cm tall. When grown commercially in a nursery, the tap root tends to coil in the bottom of the pot and is broken off when the sapling is transplanted, setting back its development severely while a replacement grows. Insufficient time is taken to preserve the tap root and most growers do not even know of its existence or purpose.

The wise gardener, when transplanting a sapling, will uncoil the tender tap root, weight its tip and carefully thread it down a long, vertical hole driven deep into the earth with a metal rod. The small amount of time invested in this process so early in the tree's life ensures its survival and will allow it to develop faster and become stronger than its commercially grown siblings. Wise business leaders use coaching to emulate the good gardener.

Universal proof of the success of new methods has been hard to demonstrate because few have understood and used them fully, and many others have been unwilling to set aside old proven ways for long enough to reap the rewards of new ones. Recently, however, as much through necessity as progress, worker participation, devolution, accountability and coaching have found their way into business language, and sometimes into behavior too.

Even if some managers were philosophically sympathetic to the Socratic method, practical models of coaching were less available than academic theses that supported the idea. Tim Gallwey was perhaps the first to demonstrate a simple but comprehensive method of coaching that could be readily applied to almost any situation. It is hardly surprising that Gallwey found himself lecturing more often to business leaders in America than to sports people, although I suspect they hoped their golf would improve too. He has just published *The Inner Game of Work*. Gallwey's earlier books did not attempt to teach coaching, but rather identified the issues we so often face in sport and business and gave clues as to how to overcome them ourselves. The coaching method was too vulnerable to distortion by the prevailing attitudes and beliefs of the would-be coach for it to be taught through a book alone, and that is a limitation of this book as well.

Many years ago I sought out Tim Gallwey, was trained by him, and founded the Inner Game in Britain. We soon formed a small team of Inner Game coaches. At first all were trained by Gallwey but later we trained our own. We ran Inner Tennis courses and Inner Skiing holidays and many golfers freed up their swings with Inner Golf. It was not long before our sporting clients began to ask us if we could apply the same methods to prevailing issues in their companies. We did, and all the leading exponents of business coaching today graduated from or were profoundly influenced by the Gallwey school of coaching.

INNER BUSINESS

Through years of experience now in the business field, we have built and elaborated on those first methods and adapted them to the issues and conditions of today's business environment. Some of us have specialized in teaching managers to coach, others have acted as independent coaches for executives and for business teams. Although we are competitors with one another in the field, we remain close friends and not infrequently work together. This in itself speaks highly of the method, for it was Tim Gallwey who suggested that your opponent in tennis is really your friend if he makes you stretch and run. He is not a friend if he just pats the ball back to you, as that will not help you to improve your game, and isn't that what we are all trying to do in our different fields?

Although Tim Gallwey, my colleagues in Performance Consultants and many others who now practice coaching in the business arena all cut our teeth in sport, coaching in sport itself has changed little overall. It remains rooted in old behavioral models and is instruction based. It is at least a decade behind in terms of the methodology of coaching in business today. That is because when we introduced coaching into business 20 years ago, the word was new to business and did not bring with it the baggage of a long history of past practice. We were able to introduce new concepts without having to fight any old ones associated with coaching.

That is not to say that we met no resistance to coaching in business; we still do at times from people who have remained strangely insulated from or blind to the changes in values, beliefs, attitudes and behaviors. Coaching as a practice in business now is here to stay, although the word itself might disappear as its associated values, beliefs, attitudes and behaviors become the norm for everyone. For the time being some definition remains in order.

MENTORING

Finally, since I am defining coaching, I should perhaps mention mentoring, another word that has crept into business parlance. The word originates from Greek mythology, in which it is reported that Odysseus, when setting out for Troy, entrusted his house and the education of his son Telemachus to his friend, Mentor. 'Tell him all you know,' Odysseus said, and thus unwittingly set some limits to mentoring.

A modern-day Mentor was Mike Sprecklen, the coach to the all-conquering rowing pair, Holmes and Redgrave. 'I was stuck, I had taught them all I knew technically,' Sprecklen said on completion of a Performance Coaching course, 'but this opens up the possibility of going further, for they can feel things that I can't even see.' He had discovered a new way forward with them, working from their experience and perceptions rather than from his own. Good coaching, and good mentoring for that matter, can and should take a performer beyond the limitations of the coach or mentor's own knowledge.

In practice and in business, mentoring has by and large come to be used interchangeably with coaching. I quote from David Clutterbuck's book *Everyone Needs a Mentor*:

In spite of the variety of definitions of mentoring (and the variety of names it is given, from coaching or counselling to sponsorship) all the experts and communicators appear to agree that it has its origins in the concept of apprenticeship, when an older, more experienced individual passed down his knowledge of how the task was done and how to operate in the commercial world.

Eric Parsloe, in his book *Coaching, Mentoring and Assessing*, does make a slight distinction by suggesting that coaching is:

directly concerned with the immediate improvement of performance and development of skills by a form of tutoring or instruction. Mentoring is always one step removed and is concerned with the longer-term acquisition of skills in a developing career by a form of advising and counselling.

I advocate an advising or counseling format as in Parsloe's mentoring, as opposed to instruction, but I apply it with equal validity and effect to immediate performance improvement and to skill development, both short and long term. It can be 'hands on' and it can be 'one step removed'; either way I call it coaching. Whether we label it coaching, advising, counseling or mentoring, if done well, its effectiveness will depend in large measure on the manager's beliefs about human potential.

The expressions 'to get the best out of someone' and 'your hidden potential' imply that more lies within the person waiting to be released. Unless the manager or coach believes that people possess more capability than they are currently expressing, he will not be able to help them express it. **He must think of his people in terms of their potential, not their performance.** The majority of appraisal systems are seriously flawed for this reason. People are put in performance boxes from which it is hard for them to escape, either in their own eyes or their manager's.

To get the best out of people, we have to believe the best is in there – but how do we know it is, how much is there, and how do we get it out? I believe it is there, not because of any scientific proof but simply from having had to find reserves I did not know I had while competing in professional sport, and from observing how people exceed all their own and others' expectations when a crisis occurs. Ordinary people like you and I will do extraordinary things when we have to. For example, who would not produce superhuman strength and courage to save their child?

The capacity is there, the crisis is the catalyst. But is crisis the only catalyst? And how long are we able to sustain extraordinary levels of performance? Some of this potential can be accessed by coaching, and performance can be sustainable, perhaps not at superhuman levels but certainly at levels far higher than we generally accept.

That our beliefs about the capability of others have a direct impact on their performance has been adequately demonstrated in a number of experiments from the field of education. In these tests teachers are told, wrongly, that a group of average pupils are either scholarship candidates or have learning difficulties. They teach a set curriculum to the group for a period of time. Subsequent academic tests show that the pupils' results invariably reflect the false beliefs of their teachers about their ability. It is equally true that the performance of employees will reflect the beliefs of their managers.

For example, Fred sees himself as having limited potential. He feels safe only when he operates well within his prescribed limit. This is like his shell. His manager will only trust him with tasks within his shell. The manager will give him task A, because he trusts Fred to do it and Fred can. The manager will not give him task B, because he sees this as beyond Fred's capability. He sees only Fred's performance, not his potential. If he gives the task to Jane instead, which is expedient and understandable, the manager reinforces or validates Fred's shell and increases its strength and thickness. He needs to do the opposite, to help Fred venture outside his shell, to support or coach him to success with task B.

To use coaching successfully we have to adopt a far more optimistic view than usual of the dormant capability of people, all people. Pretending we are optimistic is insufficient because our genuine beliefs are conveyed in many subtle ways of which we are not aware.

APPLICATION

When and where do we use coaching and for what? Here are some of the more obvious opportunities to apply coaching at work:

Motivating staff	Appraisals and assessments
Delegating	Task performance
Problem solving	Planning and reviewing
Relationship issues	Staff development
Team building	Team working

Coaching can be used proactively, during a performance or in review

The list is endless, and the opportunities can be tackled by using a highly structured approach, the formal coaching session. The coach/manager can equally choose to retain a degree of structure but be less formal – superficially it might sound like a normal conversation and the term coaching might not be used. Far more pervasive than either of these uses, and perhaps more important, are the continuous awareness and employment of the underlying principles of coaching during the many brief daily interactions that occur between manager and staff. In these cases we would not describe the interaction as coaching, and it might consist of no more than a single sentence – probably a question. However, the wording, the intention and the effect of that sentence would be different. Here is an example:

An employee, Sue, is working on a task that had been discussed and agreed with her manager the previous week. She has a problem and goes to find her manager:

SUE   I did what we agreed but it isn't working.

MANAGER   You must have done something wrong! Do it this way instead…

No coaching there, but here is an alternative based on the coaching principles:

SUE   I did what we agreed but it isn't working.

MANAGER   I just have to go and see George for a minute. See if you can find out exactly where and when the blockage occurs, and I'll be back to help you find a solution.

Ten minutes later when the manager returns:

SUE   I've got the solution, it's working fine now.

MANAGER   Great. What did you do? Did it affect anything else?

SUE   This was the problem, and I got round it like this… There are no other effects, I checked that out.

MANAGER   Sounds fine to me. See what you can do when you try!

Coaching can occur spontaneously in a minute or an hour-long session

EXAMPLE

The manager's sentence, not even a question this time although an implied one – 'See if you can find out exactly where and when the blockage occurs' – embraces the two key principles of coaching identified in Chapter 4, AWARENESS and RESPONSIBILITY. Also in this brief interaction the manager showed no blame or irritation, presented himself as a partner in the cause, and at the end reminded Sue that she had solved the problem herself and that she is more capable than she thinks.

I have argued the importance of managers recognizing the potential that lies within everyone they manage and of treating them accordingly. It is, however, even more important for people to recognize their own hidden potential. We all believe we could do better to some extent, but do we really know what we are capable of? How often do we hear or make comments such as 'Yes, she is far more capable than she thinks'?

In bold below are three revealing questions that I invite you to ask and answer, before you read the answers underneath each.

What percentage of people's potential manifests itself in the workplace on average?

Individual answers given by delegates on Performance Coaching programs range from single figures to over 70 percent, but the average for any group turns out remarkably often to be about 40 percent.

What evidence do you have to support your figure?

The three most consistent answers are:

❑ The things that people do so well outside the workplace.
❑ How well people respond in a crisis.
❑ I just know I could be much more productive.

What external and internal blocks obstruct the manifestation of the rest of that potential?

We must see people in terms of their future potential, not their past performance

The external ones most frequently cited are:

❏ The restrictive structures and practices of my company.
❏ The lack of encouragement and opportunity.
❏ The prevailing management style of the company/my boss.

The single universal internal block is unfailingly the same, variously described as fear of failure, lack of confidence, self-doubt and lack of self-belief.

I have every reason to suspect that this last answer is true. It is certainly true for me. In a safe environment people tend to tell the truth about themselves. If lack of confidence and so on is perceived to be true, then in effect it becomes the case anyway. The logical response would be to put every effort into building employees' self-belief and coaching is tailor made for that, but many business people are anything but logical when the need for a change in management behavior is raised. They far prefer to hope for, look for, pay for or even wait for a technical or structural fix, rather than adopting a human or psychological performance improvement, however straightforward it may be. There is another reason as well.

Building others' self-belief demands that we release the desire to control them or to maintain their belief in our superior abilities. One of the best things we can do for them is to assist them in surpassing us. Children's most memorable and exciting moments are often the first occasions on which they beat a parent at a game of skill. That is why in the early days we sometimes allow them to win. We want our children to overtake us and we are proud when they do – would that we could be so proud when our staff do the same! We can only gain, through their greater performance and from the satisfaction of watching them and helping them grow. However, all too often we are afraid of losing our job, our authority, our credibility or our own self-belief.

Building awareness, responsibility and self-belief is the goal of a coach

Since self-belief is key to the manifestation of potential and performance, it is imperative to build a track record of

SELF-BELIEF

The underlying intent of every coaching interaction is to build the coachee's self-belief

Self-belief is built when we make decisions, take successful actions and recognize our full responsibility for both

successes. Nothing succeeds like success. In coaching it is paramount that the coachee produces the desired results from the coaching session, without fail. It is incumbent on coaches to understand this and ensure that they have helped the coachee to optimal clarity and commitment to action, including pre-empting all obstacles. Coaches are often afraid to pursue a coachee to certain success because they fear being seen as aggressive. Nevertheless, coaching that does not result in success – and the coachee's own recognition of that success – will only cause a reduction in self-belief and undermine the primary objective of the coaching.

For people to build their self-belief, in addition to accumulating successes they need to know that their success is due to their own efforts. They must also know that other people believe in them, which means being trusted, allowed, encouraged and supported to make their own choices and decisions. It means being treated as an equal, even if their job has a lesser label. It means not being patronised, instructed, ignored, blamed, threatened or denigrated by word or deed. Unfortunately, much generally expected and accepted management behavior embodies many of these negatives and effectively lowers the self-esteem of those being managed.

Coaching is an intervention that has as its underlying and ever-present goal the building of others' self-belief, regardless of the content of the task or issue. If managers bear this principle in mind and act on it persistently and authentically, they will be staggered by the improvements in relationships and in performance that result.

Coaching is not merely a technique to be wheeled out and rigidly applied in certain prescribed circumstances. It is a way of managing, a way of treating people, a way of thinking, a way of being. Roll on the day when the word coaching disappears from our lexicon altogether, and it just becomes the way we relate to one another at work, and elsewhere too.

However, to help understand the fundamental principles of coaching, we will in the next few chapters be examining the more structured end of the spectrum. I hope that you will destructure it as you become more familiar with and practiced in the principles.

2

The Manager as Coach

A manager must be experienced as a support, not as a threat.

Here lies a paradox, because the manager traditionally holds the pay check, the key to promotion, and also the ax. This is fine so long as you believe the only way to motivate is through the judicious application of the carrot and the stick.

However, for coaching to work at its best the relationship between the coach and the coachee must be one of partnership in the endeavor, of trust, of safety and of minimal pressure. The check, the key and the ax have no place here, as they can serve only to inhibit that relationship.

CAN A MANAGER BE A COACH?

Can a manager, therefore, be a coach at all? Yes, but coaching demands the highest qualities of that manager: empathy, integrity and detachment, as well as a willingness, in most cases, to adopt a fundamentally different approach to his staff. He will also have to find his own way, for there are few role models for him to follow, and he may even have to cope with initial resistance from some of his staff, suspicious of any departure from traditional management. They may fear the additional personal responsibility implicit in a coaching style of management. These problems can be anticipated and generally are easily coached away.

The polarities of management or communication style with which we are familiar place an autocratic approach on one end of the spectrum, and *laissez faire* and hope for the best on the other.

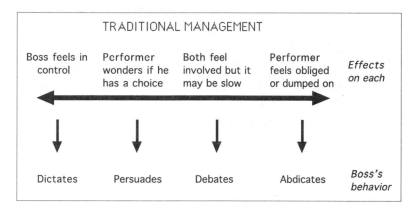

When I was a little boy, my parents told me what to do, and scolded me when I didn't. When I went to school, my teachers told me what to do, and caned me if I didn't. When I joined the army, the sergeant told me what to do, and God help me if I didn't, so I did! When I got my first job, my boss told me what to do too. So when I reached a position of some authority, what did I do? I told people what to do, because that is what all my role models had done. That is true for the majority of us: we have been brought up on telling, and we are very good at it.

DICTATES

The attraction of telling or dictating is that, besides being quick and easy, it provides the dictator with the feeling of being in control. This is, however, a fallacy. The dictator upsets and demotivates his staff, but they neither dare show it nor offer feedback, which would not have been heard anyway. The result is that they are subservient in his presence but behave differently when his back is turned, with resentment, with poor performance at best, maybe by downing tools or even by sabotage. He is anything but in control – he is deluding himself.

RECALL

There is yet another problem with the dictating end of the traditional management spectrum: the problem of recall. Quite simply, we do not remember very well something we are told. The table below is an oft-used part of training folklore, but it is so relevant that it warrants being repeated here. It was a piece of research first carried out some time ago by IBM, but it was repeated, and the results confirmed, by the UK Post Office more recently. A group of people were divided randomly into three subgroups, each of which was taught something quite simple, the same thing, using three different approaches. The results speak for themselves. One thing they show that particularly concerns us, however, is how dramatically recall declines when people are only told something.

I well remember showing this to a couple of parachute-jumping trainers who became very concerned about the fact that they taught emergency procedures only by telling. They hurried to change their system before they were faced with a terminal freefall!

	Told	Told and shown	Told, shown and experienced
Recall after 3 weeks	70%	72%	85%
Recall after 3 months	10%	32%	65%

PERSUADES

If we move along the traditional management spectrum to the right we come to selling or persuading. Here the boss lays out his good idea and attempts to convince us how great it is. We know better than to challenge him, so we smile demurely and carry out his instructions. Nicer maybe, if a bit phoney, and it gives the appearance of being more democratic. But is it really? We still end up doing exactly what the boss wants, and he gets little input from us. Nothing much has changed.

When we get further along the line to discussing, resources are genuinely pooled and the good boss may be willing to follow a path other than his own option, provided it is going in the right direction. Sir John Harvey-Jones, interviewed about team leadership for David Hemery's book *Sporting Excellence*, said:

If the direction everyone else wants is not where I thought we should go, I'll go ... once the thing is rolling, you can change direction anyway. I may see they were right or they may realize it isn't the right place to be and head towards my preferred course, or we may both come to realize that we would rather be in a third alternative. In industry, you can only move with the hearts and minds.

Attractive as democratic discussion may be, it can be time consuming and result in indecision.

The far end of the scale, just leaving the subordinate to get on with it, frees the manager for other duties and gives the subordinate freedom of choice. It is, however, risky for both. The manager has abdicated his responsibility, although the buck still stops with him, and the subordinate may perform poorly due to a lack of awareness of many aspects of the task.

Managers sometimes withdraw with good intent, wishing to force subordinates to learn to cope with more responsibility. This strategy seldom serves its purpose, because if the subordinate feels obliged to take responsibility, rather than choosing to, his personal ownership remains low and his performance will not reflect the benefit of the self-motivation that the manager hopes to generate.

The majority of managers will position themselves on the scale somewhere between these extremes, but coaching lies on a different plane altogether and combines the benefits of both ends with the risks of neither.

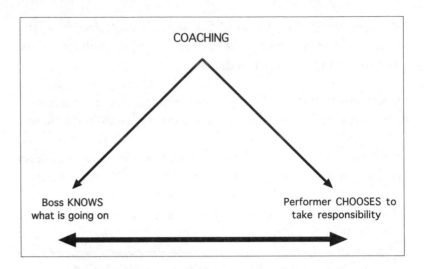

COACHING

Boss KNOWS
what is going on

Performer CHOOSES to
take responsibility

In responding to the manager's coaching questions the subordinate becomes aware of every aspect of the task and the actions necessary. This clarity enables him to envisage the near certainty of success, and so to choose to take responsibility. By listening to the answers to his coaching questions, the manager knows not only the action plan but the thinking that went into it. He is now far better informed than he would be if he told the subordinate what to do, and therefore has better control of what is going on. Since the dialog and the relationships in coaching are non-threatening and supportive, no behavior change occurs when the manager is absent. Coaching provides the manager with real not illusionary control, and provides the subordinate with real not illusory responsibility.

THE ROLE OF THE MANAGER

What this throws up is, 'What is the role of a manager?' Many managers too frequently find themselves fire-fighting, struggling to get the job done. By their own admission they are unable to devote the time they feel they should to long-term planning, to visioning, to taking the overview, to surveying alternatives, the competition, new products and the like. Most importantly, they are unable to devote the time to growing their people, to staff development. They send them on a training course or two and kid themselves that that will do it. They seldom get their money's worth.

So how can managers find the time to coach their staff? It is so much quicker to dictate. The paradoxical answer is that if they coach their staff, the developing staff shoulder much greater responsibility, freeing the manager from fire-fighting not only to coach more but to attend to those overarching issues that only he can address. So growing people is enlightened self-interest rather than idealism that offers no added value. Sure, at times it will be all hands to the pumps and to hell with the niceties, but that is acceptable and accepted in a culture in which people feel cared for.

Managers often ask me when they should coach, or at least how they should decide whether to coach or tell. The answer is quite simple.

If **time** is the predominant criterion in a situation (e.g. in an immediate crisis), doing the job yourself or telling someone else exactly what to do will probably be the fastest way.

If the **quality** of the result matters most (e.g. an artist painting a masterpiece), coaching for high awareness and responsibility is likely to deliver the most.

If maximizing the **learning** is predominant (e.g. a child doing homework), clearly coaching will optimize learning and its retention.

In most situations in the workplace, time, quality and learning all have some relevance all of the time. The sad truth is that in most businesses, time takes precedence over quality and learning is relegated to a poor third. Is it surprising that managers have such a hard time giving up telling and that business performance falls far short of what it could and should be?

If managers manage by the principles of coaching, they both get the job done to a higher standard and develop their people simultaneously. It sounds too good to be true to have 250 days a year of getting the job done and 250 days a year of staff development per person, but that is precisely what the manager/coach gets.

> A manager's task is simple — to get the job done and to grow his staff. Time and cost pressures limit the latter. Coaching is one process with both effects

> A coaching management style/culture results in getting the job done well for 250 days a year, developing people for 250 days a year, and a lot of self-belief

3
The Nature of Change

If we do not change direction, we are liable to end up where we are headed.

The demand for change in business practice has never been greater than it is today. That the traditional culture of businesses has to change has been gaining acceptance intellectually for some years, but more recently the phrase 'if they are to survive' has been added without much dissent. How has this come about? Why does what was good practice in the past not still hold good? Are we rushing into change for change's sake? How do we know it is going to be any better? And for how long?

There are plenty of cynical responses: 'We have made all these grand changes in the past and they did not make any difference.' 'No sooner will we have made this change than we will have to change again.' 'Let's do nothing, it's just another new flavor of the month.' These are the anxieties of many who are threatened by the inevitable plethora of uncertainties, but the questions and concerns are also very valid and we need to address them if we are going to manage change well.

There are also pragmatic reasons for change, such as increasing global competition forcing the pace toward leaner, more efficient, flexible and responsive units. The pace of technological innovation frequently leads to managers finding they have never learned the skills of the teams they employ. Demographic changes, the further integration of Europe and the realignment refinancing of the old Eastern bloc states pose new challenges, and globalization is upon us. Businesses are inextricably bound to the global social and psychological trends as well as the economic ones. In addition, the commercial and financial demands made by businesses, and their power, mean that they also profoundly influence the surrounding culture.

So the culture has to change – but from what and to what? The answers to this, and most of the questions above, depend more on perspective than on consensus, but any new culture will have to deliver higher levels of performance. No corporation is going to take the risks and upheavals involved in major change just for the sake of change, or merely to be nicer to employees. Culture change will be, and needs to be, performance driven. Competition demands it, and those companies and individuals who don't perform better than has been acceptable in the past won't survive in the oversubscribed, fractured, unstable markets of our world today. When the opportunities for promotion and pay increases are shrinking in most sectors, how do we drive up performance?

Expressions such as 'our people are our greatest resource', 'we must empower all our staff', 'releasing latent potential', 'downsizing and devolving responsibility' and 'getting the best out of our people' have become clichés in recent years. Their true meaning remains as valid today as when they were first coined, but all too often they are hollow words. They are talked about far more than acted on. Coaching for performance is just what it says – a means of obtaining optimum performance – but one that demands fundamental changes in attitude, in managerial behavior and in organizational structure. It gives the clichés substance.

Most of the businesses we work with approach us because they are embarked on a process of fundamental change – or

FROM WHAT TO WHAT?

at least would like to be. They have recognized that if they are to achieve real performance improvement, their managers must adopt a coaching-based management style.

NEW STYLE

These companies have already identified that coaching is the management style of a transformed culture, and that as the style changes from directing to coaching the culture of the organization will begin to change. Hierarchy gives way to support, blame gives way to honest evaluation, external motivators are replaced by self-motivation, protective barriers fall as teams build, change is no longer feared but welcomed, satisfying the boss becomes pleasing the customer. Secrecy and censorship are replaced by openness and honesty, pressure of work becomes challenging work, and short-term firefighting reactions give way to longer-term strategic thinking. These are some of the characteristics of the emerging business culture, but each business will have its own unique mix and priorities.

INVOLVEMENT

However, there is another factor, more subtle perhaps, but so pervasive that some find it hard to put their finger on. There is a growing awareness in ordinary people leading them to demand more involvement in the decisions that affect them, at work, at play, locally, nationally or even globally. Decisions made by traditional authorities, governments and other institutions, previously immune from challenge, are being called into question and sometimes brought to book by the media, pressure groups and concerned individuals. Is this not what was happening within the former Soviet Union and the Eastern bloc, which led to the collapse of communism? In our society today it is easier to get a hearing than ever before, and cracks are appearing in impregnable citadels' dubious respectability. Those that have something to hide hunker down and snarl, but the majority of thinking people welcome the changes, even if those changes do generate some feelings of insecurity. It matters not whether one sees this awareness as some evolutionary emergence, or merely the result of a world shrinking from immersion in a sea of instant communication. It is upon us either way.

PUSH TO PULL

This demand for involvement and choice is being seen as a very broad-based change in our whole society and is often described as the shift from *push* to *pull*. What do we mean by this? Perhaps the answer is best illustrated by an example.

We all receive commercial and charitable junk mail that we don't want, resent and regard as an intrusion. Some of us are on more mailing lists than others and some resent it more than others. As you may have guessed, I am one of the latter! The advent of the internet gave us access to what we want when we want it. We have more choice. We *pull* off the internet what we want, instead of constantly having to bin what is *pushed* through our mail box. Would it were that simple, of course. When I retrieve my emails or go on to the internet, I often find that the pushers have got there first and up pops some wretched dancing advertisement before I can grab the mouse.

I can recall when we only had two television channels in the UK; now we are spoiled for choice. We can select among hundreds of channels and even in some cases choose which camera to follow in a sports event. This again reflects the shift from push to pull. It is a result of the demand for choice in viewing, but we still have to put up with pushy commercials.

A similar shift is occurring in managing people. You used to be able to tell or push people to do what you want, but now they expect and demand to be treated differently. This is not a retrogade step as some diehard pushers would have us believe. It is the evolving consciousness of our collective society, for which we should be grateful as it holds the promise of higher performance possibilities. Deep down people want choice and responsibility, and in many cases they are getting these. Nevertheless, although executives talk about empowering people all the time, they still have plenty of push left in them.

Responsibility demands choice. Choice implies freedom. People, ordinary people, are beginning to recognize not only that this is what they want, but that it can be had to a far greater extent than previously understood even within our complex variety of social structures. Instead of being threatened by this, managers should realize that they can capitalize on it, give people responsibility, and that they in turn will give of their best. This way everyone wins.

BLAME CULTURE

Blame evokes defensiveness – defensiveness reduces awareness

There is much talk in companies today about getting rid of the 'blame culture' – and almost no action. Blame is endemic to business, and endemic to a dictating philosophy. Blame is about history, fear and the past. We need to refocus on aspiration, hope and the future. Not only does the fear of blame inhibit even the most calculated risk taking, it blocks honest recognition, identification and acknowledgment of inefficiencies in a system. Appropriate corrections cannot be put in place without this crucial accurate feedback. Fundamental culture change will not happen if blame comes along too. Most businesses, and most people, will have great difficulty leaving it behind.

STRESS

There is another good reason for increasing responsibility at work. Work-related stress, in the US at least, is said to be reaching epidemic levels. A recent survey conducted by an independent research company in Minneapolis revealed that the leading cause of burnout was 'little personal control allowed' in doing one's job and that this was prevalent at all times irrespective of the economy. This in itself suggests an urgent need for change toward working practices that encourage personal responsibility.

But what is the reason for this correlation between stress and personal control? Self-esteem is the life force of the personality, and if that is suppressed or diminished so is the person. Stress results from long periods of suppression. Offering someone choice and control wherever possible in the workplace acknowledges and validates their capability and their self-esteem. Stress is thereby eliminated.

FEAR OF CHANGE

However, for many people the fear of change, any change, looms large. This is not surprising when you consider that there is little we can do to prepare our children for the world they are going to live in. It certainly won't be as we have known it, but we don't know how it *will* be. Perhaps all we can hope to teach them is the flexibility and adaptability to cope with what will be.

Most of what our great-grandparents taught their children would hold good throughout their lives. By and large they lived in a stable state, or at least stability was the accepted norm even if that was beginning to change! Most of us were brought up with that stable state mentality, but we are having to adapt to conditions that seem anything but stable. Our grandchildren will have grown up with change as their norm, so all they will have to cope with is the varying pace of that change. We are the generation struggling to adjust to the fact that change is now the norm because our teeth were cut on the illusion of stability. When much of what we know and love is in flux, full acceptance of personal responsibility becomes a physical and psychological necessity for survival.

CHANGE AS THE NORM

4

The Nature of Coaching

Building AWARENESS and RESPONSIBILITY is the essence of good coaching.

Some readers may think by now that I have departed far from the subject of coaching, and that the role of the manager and the context of change are side issues. They are not. They are the context of coaching. If they are not understood, coaching becomes merely another tool in a kitbag of quick fixes. It is possible to coach another person to solve a problem or learn a new skill by diligently applying the coaching method and sequence described in this book without agreeing with the underlying coaching philosophy. The coaching may be competent and may achieve limited success, but it will fall far short of what is possible.

Some coaches have started that way. I well remember one ski instructor we trained who was simply unready for the deeper understanding. His manner was autocratic, dogmatic and somewhat manipulative, but by systematically applying our method to skiing he got results that in turn served to convince him that offering the learner more choice was one key to unlocking all kinds of hidden potential. He soon changed his whole philosophy on and off the slopes. Not only did he go on to write a self-coaching ski manual, and to design the best skiing program I know, but he became an expert coach in the field of sales training.

RAISING AWARENESS

The first key element of coaching is AWARENESS, which is the product of focused attention, concentration and clarity. Let us return for a moment to the *Concise Oxford Dictionary*: aware means 'conscious, not ignorant, having knowledge'. I prefer what *Webster* adds: 'aware implies having knowledge of something through alertness in observing or in interpreting what one sees, hears, feels, etc.' Like our eyesight or our hearing, both of which can be good or poor, there are infinite degrees of awareness. Unlike eyesight or hearing, in which the norm is good, the norm of our everyday awareness is rather poor. A magnifying glass or an amplifier can raise our sight and hearing threshold way above normal. In the same way, awareness can be raised or heightened considerably by focused attention and by practice without having to resort to the corner drugstore! Increased awareness gives greater clarity of perception than normal, as does a magnifying glass.

While awareness includes seeing and hearing in the workplace, it encompasses much more than that. It is the gathering and the clear perception of the relevant facts and information, and the ability to determine what is relevant. That ability will include an understanding of systems, of dynamics, of relationships between things and people and inevitably some understanding of psychology. Awareness also encompasses self-awareness, in particular recognizing when and how emotions or desires distort one's own perception.

In the development of physical skills the awareness of bodily sensations may be crucial. In the majority of sports, for example, the most effective way to increase individual physical efficiency is for the performer to become

I am able to control only that of which I am aware. That of which I am unaware controls me. AWARENESS empowers me

AWARENESS LEADS TO SKILL

No two human minds or bodies are the same. How can I tell you how to use yours to their best? Only you can discover how, with AWARENESS

If there was only the right way to do something, Fosbury would never have flopped and Björn Borg would never have won Wimbledon

increasingly aware of the physical sensations during an activity. This is poorly understood by the majority of sports coaches, who persist in imposing their technique from outside. When kinesthetic awareness is focused on a movement, the immediate discomforts and corresponding inefficiencies in the movement are reduced and soon eliminated. The result is a more fluid and efficient form that corresponds more closely to the 'book' technique, with the important advantage that it is geared to the particular performer's body rather than the 'average' body that the book addresses.

A teacher, instructor or for that matter a manager will be tempted to show and tell others to do something in the way he himself was taught to do it, or the way 'the book' says it should be done. In other words, he teaches the student or subordinate his way and thereby perpetuates conventional wisdom. While the learning and employment of the standard or 'right' way to do something will show initial performance benefits, the personal preferences and attributes of the performer are suppressed, making life simpler for the manager. The performer's dependence on the expert is also maintained, which boosts the manager's ego and his illusion of power.

The coaching alternative of awareness raising surfaces and highlights the unique attributes of body and mind of each individual, while at the same time building the ability and the confidence to improve without another's prescription. It builds self-reliance, self-belief/confidence and self-responsibility. Coaching should never be confused with 'here are the tools, go and find out for yourself'. Our own normal level of awareness is relatively low. Left to our own devices we are liable to take an age to reinvent the wheel and/or to develop only partially effective methods that can consolidate into bad habits. So the awareness-raising function of the expert coach is indispensable – at least until or unless we develop the skill of self-coaching, which opens the door to continuous self-improvement and self-discovery.

What we need to increase our awareness of will vary. Each activity is geared to different parts of ourselves. Sport is primarily physical, but some sports are highly visual too. Musicians require and develop high levels of auditory awareness. Sculptors and magicians need tactile awareness, and business people require mental and people awareness but certainly other areas too.

Although all this explanation of awareness may seem daunting at first, it is something that develops quickly through simple practice and application, and through being coached. It is perhaps easier to relate to the following lay definitions:

❑ Awareness is knowing what is happening around you.
❑ Self-awareness is knowing what you are experiencing.

Another term may add to our understanding of what we mean by awareness: INPUT. Every human activity can be reduced to INPUT—PROCESS—OUTPUT.

INPUT

For example, when you drive to work, you receive input in the form of other traffic movements, road and weather conditions, changing speed and spatial relationships, the sounds of your engine, your instruments and the comfort, tension or tiredness in your body. This is all input that you may welcome, reject, take on board sufficiently, receive in its intricate detail, or not even notice save for its major elements.

You may consciously be aware of your driving, or unconsciously acquire the input necessary to drive safely to work, while you listen to the *Today Programme* on the radio. Either way you are receiving input. Better drivers will receive a higher quality and quantity of input, which provides them with more accurate and detailed information that they process and act on to produce the appropriate output, the speed and position of the vehicle on the road.

However good you are at processing the input received and acting on it, the quality of your output will depend on the quality and quantity of the input. Awareness raising is the act of sharpening the acuity of our input receptors, often tuning our senses but also engaging our brain.

While high awareness is vital for high performance, we are blessed with a mechanism that continually seeks to lower our awareness to the level of 'just enough to get by'. While this sounds unfortunate, it is in fact essential if we are to avoid getting into input overload. The downside is that if we do not raise our awareness and that of those with whom we work, we will deliver output at a minimal level. The skill of the coach is to raise and sustain awareness at the appropriate level and in those areas where it is required.

On our courses we define awareness as **high-quality relevant input**. We could add the word **self-generated** before it, but in a sense that is already implied because input will simply not be high quality unless it is self-generated. The act of becoming engaged in something itself provides the quality. Consider the poverty of the image you receive if I say, 'The flowers out there are red', compared to the input you get when I ask you, 'What color are the flowers out there?' and you are compelled to see for yourself. Better still if I ask what tone or shade of red they are.

One way gives a standard flower image, the other a detailed explosion of life in a myriad of subtle shades of red as it is at a particular instant. It is unique. In fifteen minutes it will be different, for the sun will have moved. It will never be quite the same again. So self-generated input is infinitely richer, more immediate, more real.

Another word that characterizes awareness is **feedback** – feedback from the environment, from your body, from your actions, from the equipment you are using, as opposed to feedback from other people.

Higher than normal focused attention leads to higher than normal performance

Change follows naturally and unforced once quality feedback or input is received

RESPONSIBILITY

RESPONSIBILITY is the other key concept or goal of coaching. In the last chapter I raised the issue of the relationship between business culture change and a growing concern for accountability and responsibility, both collectively and individually. Responsibility is also crucial for high performance. When we truly accept, choose or take

If I give you my advice and it fails, you will blame me. I have traded my advice for your responsibility and that is seldom a good deal

responsibility for our thoughts and our actions, our commitment to them rises and so does our performance. When we are ordered to be responsible, told to be, expected to be or even given responsibility, if we do not fully accept it performance does not rise. Sure, we may do the job because there is an implied threat if we do not, but doing something to avoid a threat does not optimize performance. To feel truly responsible invariably involves choice. Let's look at a couple of examples.

BLAME

If I give you advice, especially if it is unsolicited, and you take the action but it fails, what will you do? Blame me, of course, which is a clear indication of where you see the responsibility lying. The failure might even be attributable as much to your lack of ownership as to my bad advice. In the workplace, when the advice is a command, ownership is at zero and this can lead to resentment, surreptitious sabotage, or ownership of the reverse action. *You gave me no choice; you damaged my self-esteem; I cannot recover that through an action of which I have no ownership, so I take responsibility for an alternative action that will damage you. Of course, that course of action may damage me too, but at least I will have got my own back!* If this (unconscious) sequence in italics seems exaggerated to you, let me assure you that there are millions of workers with bad employers who would acknowledge having followed that track at times.

Here is another example of the difference between the normal or imposed level of responsibility and high or chosen responsibility. Imagine a group of construction workers being briefed:

CHOICE

'Fred, go and get a ladder. There's one in the shed.'

What does Fred do if he finds no ladder there? He returns and says, 'There's no ladder there.'

What if I had asked instead, 'We need a ladder. There's one in the shed. Who is willing to get it?'

Fred replies 'I will', but when he gets there there is no ladder. What will he do this time? He will look elsewhere – but why? Because he feels responsible. He wants to succeed. He will find a ladder for his own sake, his own self-esteem. What I did differently was to give him a choice, to which he responded.

One of our clients had a history of poor labor relations. In an attempt to improve these I ran a series of courses for shopfloor supervisors. Although the company grapevine had it that our course was very enjoyable, the participants were invariably suspicious, defensive, even resistant at the outset. I recognized that their pattern was to resist anything senior managers told them to do. They had been told to attend the course, and they would resist that too.

To defuse this unproductive situation, I asked them how much choice they had had about attending the course.

'None,' they chorused.

Self-belief, self-motivation, choice, clarity, commitment, awareness, responsibility and action are the products of coaching

'Well, you have a choice now,' I said. 'You have met your obligation to the company – you're here. Congratulations! Now, here is your choice. How do you want to spend these two days? You can learn as much as possible, you can resist, you can be as inattentive as you like, you can fool around. Write a sentence describing what you choose to do. You can keep it to yourself, if you prefer, or share it with your neighbor. I don't need to know and I won't tell your boss what you do. The choice is yours.'

The atmosphere in the room was transformed. There was something like a collective sigh of relief, but also a release of energy, and the vast majority then engaged at a high level of involvement. Choice and responsibility can work wonders.

These simple examples clearly illustrate how important choice is for the performance gain that occurs with full responsibility. That does not occur unless the person feels responsible. *Telling* someone to be responsible for something doesn't make them *feel* responsible for it. They may fear failure and feel guilty if they do fail, but that is not the same as feeling responsible. That comes with choice, which in turn demands a question. We will look at the construction of coaching questions in the next chapter.

AWARENESS and RESPONSIBILITY are without doubt two qualities that are crucial to performance in any activity. My colleague David Hemery, 400-meter hurdler and 1968 Olympic gold medalist, researched 63 of the world's top performers from more than 20 different sports for his book *Sporting Excellence*. In spite of considerable variations in other areas, AWARENESS and RESPONSIBILITY consistently appeared to be the two most important attitudinal factors common to all – and the attitude or the state of mind of the performer is the key to performance of any kind.

THE MIND IS KEY

For his research, David Hemery asked each of the performers to what extent they thought the mind was involved in playing their sport. David wrote, 'The unanimous verdict was couched in words like "immensely", "totally", "that's the whole game", "you play with your mind", "that's where the body movement comes from". And as a minimum, "It's equal to the body."' Top performance in business demands no less. The mind is key.

The mind is key – but where is the key to the mind?

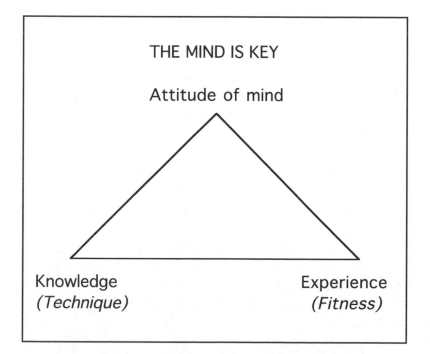

THE MIND IS KEY

Attitude of mind

Knowledge
(Technique)

Experience
(Fitness)

Knowledge and experience may be the business equivalents of sporting technique and physical fitness. Neither guarantees a place at the top, and many successful people have proved that neither is indispensable. A winning mind is essential.

THE WINNING MIND

A decade or so ago technical ability and fitness commensurate with your sport were what coaches worked on. The mind was not universally recognized to be so crucial, but in any case that was what the performer was born with and the coach could not do much about it. Wrong! They could and did affect the state of mind of their performers, but largely unwittingly and often negatively by their autocratic methods and obsession with technique.

The elimination of internal obstacles often diminishes external obstacles to manageable proportions

These coaches denied their performers' responsibility by telling them what to do; they denied their awareness by telling them what they saw. They withheld RESPONSIBILITY and killed AWARENESS. Some so-called coaches still do, as do many managers. They contribute to the performers' or employees' limitations as well as to their successes. The problem is that they may still get reasonable results from those they manage, so they are not motivated to try anything else, and never know or believe what they could achieve by other means.

Coaching for awareness and responsibility works in the short term for achiving a task, or in the long term for a better quality of life

In recent years much has changed in sport and most top teams employ sports psychologists to provide performers with attitudinal training. If old coaching methods remain unchanged, however, the coach will frequently be unintentionally negating the psychologist's efforts. The best way to develop and maintain the ideal state of mind for performance is to build AWARENESS and RESPONSIBILITY continuously throughout the daily practice and the skill-acquisition process. This requires a shift in the method of coaching, a shift from instruction to real coaching.

The coach is not a problem solver, a teacher, an adviser, an instructor or even an expert; he or she is a sounding board, a facilitator, a counselor, an awareness raiser. At least these words should help you to understand what the role implies.

QUALITIES OF A COACH

On our coaching courses we ask participants to list the qualities of an ideal coach. The following is a typical list and one with which I agree:

❑ Patient
❑ Detached
❑ Supportive
❑ Interested
❑ Good listener
❑ Perceptive
❑ Aware
❑ Self-aware
❑ Attentive
❑ Retentive

Often the list also contains some of the following:

❑ Technical expertise
❑ Knowledge
❑ Experience
❑ Credibility
❑ Authority

I am less in agreement with these last five and I pose a question: does a coach need to have experience or technical knowledge in the area in which he is coaching? The answer is no – not if the coach is truly acting as a detached awareness raiser. If, however, the coach does not fully believe in what he espouses, i.e. the potential of the performer and the value of self-responsibility, then he will think that he needs expertise in the subject to be able to coach. I am not suggesting that there is never a place for expert input, but the less good coach will tend to overuse it and thereby reduce the value of his coaching, because every time input is provided the responsibility of the coachee is reduced.

COACH AS EXPERT

THE PITFALLS OF KNOWLEDGE

The ideal would seem to be an expert coach with a wealth of technical knowledge too. It is, however, very hard for experts to withhold their expertise sufficiently to coach well. Let me illustrate this further with an example from tennis. Many years ago several of our Inner Tennis courses were so overbooked that we ran out of trained Inner Tennis coaches. We brought in two Inner Ski coaches, dressed them in tennis coach's uniform, put a racket under their arms and let them loose with the promise that they would not attempt to use the racket under any circumstances.

Not entirely to our surprise, the coaching job they performed was largely indistinguishable from that of their tennis-playing colleagues. However, on a couple of notable occasions they actually did better. On reflection the reason became clear. The tennis coaches were seeing the participants in terms of their technical faults; the ski coaches, who could not recognize such faults, saw the participants in terms of the efficiency with which they used their bodies. Body inefficiency stems from self-doubt and inadequate body awareness. The ski coaches, having to rely on the participants' own self-diagnosis, were therefore tackling problems at cause, whereas the tennis coaches were only tackling the symptom, the technical fault. This obliged us to do more training with the tennis coaches to enable them to detach themselves more effectively from their expertise.

A LEVEL DEEPER

Let us look at the same thing with a simple example from a business context. A manager saw that her subordinate, George, did not communicate sufficiently with his colleagues in the next department, and knew that a weekly progress memo was the solution. Such a memo, however, would contain inadequate information so long as George's resistance to communicating with them persisted. Instead of being satisfied with George's agreement to send memos, the manager coached George to discover and let go of his own resistance. The lack of communication was the symptom, but the resistance was the cause. **Problems can only be resolved at the level beneath that at which they manifest themselves.**

It is hard, but by no means impossible, for an expert to be a good coach. Of course, the expertise is invaluable for many other aspects of a manager's function, and the truth is that the manager is most likely to be an expert anyway. But take the case of a senior manager in an organization that computerizes a part of its operations. If he is a good coach he should have no difficulty coaching his staff to develop their computer skills further, whether he understands the new system or not. As soon as he does this, any credibility gap that may exist in the minds of some of his staff will soon disappear, and he will be able to retain command of that department. As skills become more specialized and technically complex, coaching may be an absolute prerequisite for managers.

THE MANAGER – EXPERT OR COACH?

Our potential is realized by optimizing our own individuality and uniqueness, never by molding them to another's opinion of what constitutes best practice

5
Effective Questions

Telling or asking closed questions saves people from having to think.
Asking open questions causes them to think for themselves.

*I*n the previous chapter it became clear that it is questions that best generate AWARENESS and RESPONSIBILITY. It would be easy if any old question would do, but it won't. We need to examine the effectiveness of various types of question. To do so I will use a simple analogy from sport. Ask anyone what is the most frequently used instruction in any ball sport, and they will tell you 'Keep your eye on the ball.'

In all ball sports it is certainly very important to watch the ball, but does the command 'Watch the ball' actually cause you to do so? No. If it did, many more of us would be far better at our sport. We all know that a golfer hits balls further and straighter when he is relaxed, but will the command 'Relax' cause him to feel more relaxed? No, it will probably make him more tense.

If commanding a person to do what they need to do does not produce the desired effect, what does? Let's try a question.

❏ **'Are you watching the ball?'** How would we respond to that? Defensively, perhaps, and we would probably lie, just as we did at school when the teacher asked us if we were paying attention.

❏ **'Why are you not watching the ball?'** More defensiveness – or perhaps a little analysis if you are that way inclined. 'I am', 'I don't know', 'because I was thinking about my grip' or, more truthfully, 'because you are distracting me and making me nervous'.

These are not very effective questions, but consider the effect of the following:

❏ **'Which way is the ball spinning as it comes towards you?'**
❏ **'How high is it this time as it crosses the net?'**
❏ **'Does it spin faster or slower after it bounces, this time – each time?'**
❏ **'How far is it from your opponent when you first see which way it is spinning?'**

These questions are of an altogether different order. They create four important effects that neither the other questions nor commands do:

❏ This type of question **compels the player** to watch the ball. It is not possible to answer the question unless he or she does that.
❏ The player will have to **focus to a higher order** than normal to give the accurate answer the question demands, providing a higher quality of input.
❏ The answers sought are **descriptive not judgmental**, so there is no risk of descent into self-criticism or damage to self-esteem.
❏ We have the benefit of a **feedback loop for the coach** who is able to verify the accuracy of the player's answer, and therefore the quality of concentration.

This leads one to wonder why all those sports coaches persist in giving such an ineffective command as 'Keep your eye on the ball'. There are probably two main reasons: they have never considered whether it works or not, because it has always been done that way; and they are more concerned about what they say than its effect on their pupil.

THE HEART OF COACHING

I have taken some time to explore this apparently straightforward act of watching a ball in order to illustrate by simple analogy the very heart of coaching. We must understand the effect we are trying to create – AWARENESS and RESPONSIBILITY – and what we have to say/do to create that effect. Just demanding what we want is useless – we must ask effective questions.

Coaching provokes proactive, focused thought, attention and observation

Similar questions also focus attention and evoke clarity in business. 'What is the current stock?' 'What is the most difficult issue for you?' 'When is the engineer going to arrive?' 'In what way will this price change affect our most recent customers?' All these are specific questions that demand specific answers.

These examples are probably sufficient to convince you that AWARENESS and RESPONSIBILITY are better raised by asking than by telling. It follows therefore that the primary form of verbal interaction from a good coach is in the interrogative. Now we need to examine how to construct the most effective kinds of questions.

THE FUNCTION OF QUESTIONS

Questions are most commonly asked in order to elicit information. I may require information to resolve an issue for myself, or if I am proffering advice or a solution to someone else. If I am a coach, however, the answers are of secondary importance. The information is not for me to make use of and may not have to be complete. I only need to know that the coachee has the necessary information. The answers given by the coachee frequently indicate to the coach the line to follow with subsequent questions, while at the same time enabling him to monitor whether the coachee is following a productive track, or one that is in line with the purpose or company objectives.

OPEN QUESTIONS

OPEN questions requiring descriptive answers promote awareness, whereas CLOSED questions are too absolute for accuracy, and YES or NO answers close the door on the exploration of further detail. They do not even compel someone to engage their brain. Open questions are much more effective for generating AWARENESS and RESPONSIBILITY in the coaching process.

The most effective questions for raising AWARENESS and RESPONSIBILITY begin with words that seek to quantify or gather facts, words like WHAT, WHEN, WHO, HOW MUCH, HOW MANY. WHY is discouraged since it often implies criticism and evokes defensiveness, and WHY and HOW, if unqualified, both cause analytical thinking, which can be counterproductive. Analysis (thinking) and awareness (observation) are dissimilar mental modes that are virtually impossible to employ simultaneously to full effect. If the accurate reporting of facts is called for, analysis of their import and meaning is better temporarily suspended. If we do need to ask such questions, WHY questions are better expressed as 'What were the reasons. . .?' and HOW questions as 'What are the steps. . .?' They evoke more specific, factual answers.

INTERROGATIVE WORDS

Questions should begin broadly and focus increasingly on detail. This demand for more detail maintains the focus and the interest of the coachee. The point is well illustrated by the exercise of looking at a square foot of carpet. After observing the pile, color, pattern and perhaps a spot or a stain, the carpet will hold little further interest for the observer and his attention will begin to wander to more interesting things. Give him a magnifying glass and he will look again in greater depth and for longer before becoming bored. A microscope could turn that little piece of carpet into a fascinating universe of forms, textures, colors, microbes and even live bugs sufficient to hold the eye and mind of the observer transfixed for many minutes more.

So it is in business coaching. The coach needs to probe deeper or for more detail to keep the coachee involved and to bring into his consciousness those often partially obscured factors that may be important.

FOCUS ON DETAIL

AREAS OF INTEREST

How, then, does the coach determine what aspects of an issue are important, especially if it is in an area about which he is not particularly knowledgeable? The principle is that questions should follow the interest and the train of thought of the coachee, not of the coach. If the coach leads the direction of the questions he will undermine the responsibility of the coachee. But what if the direction in which he is going is a dead end or a distraction? Trust that the coachee will soon find that out for himself.

If coachees are not allowed to explore avenues in which they have an interest, the fascination is likely to persist and cause distortions or diversions in the work itself, rather than merely in the coaching session. Once they have explored their interests, they will be far more present and focused on whatever will emerge as the best path. Paradoxically it may also be valuable for the coach to focus on any aspect that the coachee appears to be avoiding. So as not to break the trust and the responsibility of the coachee, this avenue of exploration is best entered into by a statement followed by a question: 'I notice that you have not mentioned... Is there any particular reason for this?'

BLIND SPOTS

Golfers and tennis players might be interested in the physical parallel to this principle. A coach might ask a pupil which part of his swing or stroke he finds most difficult to feel or be accurately aware of. It is most likely that in this 'blind spot' lies a suppressed discomfort or flaw in the movement. As the coach seeks more and more awareness in that area, the feeling is restored and the correction occurs naturally without resort to technical input from the coach. The curative properties of awareness are legion!

LEADING QUESTIONS

Leading questions, the resort of many poor coaches, indicate that the coach does not believe in what he is attempting to do. This will be quickly recognized by the coachee, and trust and the value of the coaching session will be reduced. Better for the coach to tell the coachee that he has a suggestion rather than attempt to manipulate him in that direction. Also questions that imply criticism should be avoided, such as 'Why on earth did you do that?'

BE ATTENTIVE TO ANSWERS

The coach must be fully attentive to coachees' answers to questions. Trust will be lost if he isn't, but also he will not know the best question to ask next. It must be a spontaneous process. Questions prepared mentally before they are asked will disrupt the flow and not follow the interest of the coachee. If the coach is working out the next question while the coachee is speaking, the coachee will be aware that he is not really listening. Far better to hear the person through and then pause if necessary while the next appropriate question comes to mind.

'Are there any other problems?' invites the answer 'No.' 'What other problems might there be?' invites more thought

Most people are not good at listening to others; we are told to listen at school, not trained to, or coached to. It is a skill that requires concentration and practice. Yet strangely enough few people have difficulty listening to the news or to a good radio play. Interest holds the attention; perhaps we need to learn to be interested in others. When we really do listen to someone, or when someone really listens to us, how appreciated it is. When we listen, do we really hear? When we look, do we really see? We short-change ourselves and those we coach if we do not really hear and see them, and by that I mean maintain eye contact with them. Obsession with our own thoughts and opinions and the compulsion to talk, particularly if one is placed in any kind of advisory role, are strong. It has been said that since we were given two ears and one mouth, we should listen twice as much as we speak. Perhaps the hardest thing a coach has to learn to do is to shut up!

TONE OF VOICE

What do we listen to and for? The coachee's tone of voice will indicate any emotion and should be listened to. A monotone may indicate repetition of an old line of thought, a more animated voice will indicate the awakening of new ideas. The coachee's choice of words can be very revealing: a predominance of negative terms, a shift toward formality or childish language all have hidden meaning that can help the coach to understand and therefore facilitate effectively.

BODY LANGUAGE

As well as listening the coach needs to watch the coachee's body language, not with the purpose of making glib observations but again to help with the choice of question. The coachee's high level of interest in the direction of the coaching may well be indicated by a forward posture. Uncertainty or anxiety in answers may be revealed by his hand partially covering his mouth while speaking. Arms folded across the chest often indicate resistance or defiance, and an open body posture suggests receptivity and flexibility. I am not going to go into the many aspects of body language here, but one guide is that if the words say one thing and the body seems to be saying something else, the body is more likely to indicate the true feelings.

REFLECTING BACK

So there are listening, hearing, watching and understanding, and the coach needs to be self-aware enough to know which he is doing. However clear the coach may feel, it is worth reflecting back to the coachee from time to time and summarizing points. This will ensure correct understanding and reassure the coachee that he is being fully heard and understood. It also gives him a second chance to check on the veracity of what he has said. In most coaching sessions someone needs to take notes, but this can be agreed between the coach and the coachee. When I am coaching I like to take the notes so the coachee is free to reflect.

SELF-AWARENESS

Finally, a good coach will be applying his own self-awareness to monitor carefully his reactions, of emotion or judgment, to any of the coachee's responses, including those to him personally, that might interfere with the coach's necessary objectivity and detachment. Our own psychological history and prejudices – and no one is free of either – will influence our communication.

TRANSFERENCE

Projection and transference are the terms given to these psychological distortions that all those who teach, guide, coach or manage others need to learn to recognize and minimize. Projection means projecting on to, or perceiving in, another person one's own positive or negative traits or qualities. Transference is 'the displacement of patterns of feelings and behavior, originally experienced with significant figures of one's childhood, to individuals in one's current relationships'. In the workplace one of the most common manifestations of this is authority transference.

In any perceived hierarchical relationship, manager/subordinate or even coach/coachee, both parties' issues or unconscious feelings about authority will be operating. For example, many people give away their power to the designated authority – 'he knows, has all the answers, is more advanced' etc. – and make themselves small and childlike in the face of it. This might serve the wishes of an autocratic manager for dominance and dependency on him, but it works against the objective of coaching, which is to generate responsibility in the managed.

Another common example of an unconscious transference reaction to authority is that of rebellion and covert sabotage of the work goals. Individual transference will increase the collective frustrations and feelings of powerlessness wherever management style limits choice. One major motor manufacturer used to be able to assess the state of labor relations from the percentage of good parts dumped into the reject bins alongside the assembly line.

COUNTERTRANSFERENCE

Countertransference, which is a further complication of transference, occurs when the person in authority, manager or coach, himself unconsciously reacts to the transference from his own history by perpetuating the dependence or the rebellion. A good manager or coach will recognize his potential for this and compensate for the effects of all manifestations of transference by consciously working to empower the subordinate or coachee. If he does not, these distortions will creep into managerial or coaching relationships, with the long-term effect of seriously undermining what his management style is intended to achieve.

HELPFUL QUESTIONS

Coaching questions compel attention for an answer, focus attention for precision and create a feedback loop. Instructing does none of these

Here are a few of the questions that I consistently find to be helpful in coaching. You might want to accumulate your own from your coaching experience. Above all, they must be authentic.

❑ 'What else?' used at the end of most answers will evoke more. Plain silence, while allowing a coach to think, often evokes more too.

❑ 'If you knew the answer what would it be?' is not as daft as it sounds, since it enables the coachee to look beyond the blockage.

❑ 'What would the consequences of that be for you or for others?'

❑ 'What criteria are you using?'

❑ 'What is the hardest/most challenging part of this for you?'

❑ 'What advice would you give to a friend in your situation?'

❑ 'Imagine having a dialog with the wisest person you know or can think of. What would he or she tell you to do?'

❑ 'I don't know where to go next with this. Where would you go?'

❑ 'What would you gain/lose by doing/saying that?'

❑ 'If someone said/did that to you, what would you feel/think/do?'

6
The Sequence of Questioning

So far we have established the essential nature of AWARENESS and RESPONSIBILITY for learning and for performance improvement. We have looked at the context of coaching, at the parallels between coaching and managing, and at company culture and change. We have explored the role and the attitude of the coach, and we have considered questions as his primary form of communication. We now have to determine what to ask questions about, and in what sequence to ask them.

FORMAL OR INFORMAL?

It is important at this point to stress that coaching can be loose and informal, so much so that the coachees do not know they are being coached. For the everyday management function of briefing and debriefing staff, nothing is better than coaching, but it should not be identified as such; it would just be managing. In this case coaching ceases to be a tool of management and simply becomes the way to manage people, in my opinion the most effective way. At the other end of the spectrum, a coaching session can be scheduled and structured in such a way that the purpose and the roles are unambiguous. While the majority of coaching is of the former type, we will examine the latter in detail because, while the process is the same, the stages are more sharply defined.

ONE TO ONE

For reasons of simplicity and clarity we will look at one-to-one coaching, although the format of team coaching or even self-coaching remains exactly the same. Both of these will be elaborated in later chapters. One-to-one coaching may take place between peers, between a manager and a subordinate, between an erstwhile teacher and a student, between a coach and a performer, or between a counselor and someone seeking their assistance. One-to-one coaching can even be used in an upward direction, although generally covertly, by an employee on his boss. After all, as no one gets very far by telling his boss what to do, coaching upward has a much higher success rate!

GROW

So the sequence of questions I suggest would follow four distinct headings:

- ❏ GOAL setting for the session as well as short and long term.
- ❏ REALITY checking to explore the current situation.
- ❏ OPTIONS and alternative strategies or courses of action.
- ❏ WHAT is to be done, WHEN, by WHOM and the WILL to do it.

This sequence assumes that it is desirable to visit all four stages, which is usually the case when tackling a new issue for the first time. Often, however, coaching will be used to progress a task or process that has been discussed before or is already under way. In such cases coaching may begin and end with any stage.

It may seem strange to set GOALS before examining the REALITY. Superficial logic suggests the opposite, as we surely need to know the reality before we can set any goal. Not so – goals based on current reality alone are liable to be negative, a response to a problem, limited by past performance, lacking in creativity due to simple extrapolation, in smaller increments than what may be achievable, or even counterproductive. Short-term fixed goals may even lead us away from long-term goals. My experience with goal setting on team-training courses is that teams invariably set goals based on what has been done before rather than on what can be done in future. In many cases they make no attempt to calculate what might be possible.

Goals formed by ascertaining the ideal long-term solution, and then determining realistic steps toward that ideal, are generally far more inspiring, creative and motivating. Let me illustrate this very important point with an example. If we set about trying to solve a problem of heavy traffic volume on an important route by exploring the reality, we are likely to set goals based solely on relieving existing traffic flow, such as widening a road. This might actually run counter to a more visionary long-term goal, which would be formed by identifying the ideal traffic pattern for the region at some time in the future, and then looking at the stages needed to move in that direction.

So my suggestion is, in most circumstances, to use the sequence suggested above.

MORE THAN GROW

This sequence conveniently forms the mnemonic G R O W, to which I will refer frequently. I must stress, however, and I will repeat often, that G R O W, without the context of AWARENESS and RESPONSIBILITY and the skill of questioning to generate them, has little value. Mnemonics abound in the training business. There is S P I N, there are S M A R T goals, there is G R I T and there is G R O W coaching. These are occasionally presented or misperceived as panaceas to all business ills. They are nothing of the sort; they are only as valuable as the context in which they are used, and the context of G R O W is AWARENESS and RESPONSIBILITY.

An autocratic boss might charge his employees in the following way:

My GOAL is to sell one thousand widgets this month.

The REALITY is that you did poorly last month with only 400 sold. You are a bunch of lazy so-and-sos. Our principal competitor has a better product, so you have to try harder.

I have considered all the OPTIONS and we are not going to increase our advertising or repackage the product.

WHAT you WILL do is the following…

He has followed the G R O W model to the letter but he has not asked a single question. He has created no AWARENESS and, although he thinks he has threatened his staff into taking RESPONSIBILITY, this is not so, because they had no choice.

CONTEXT AND FLEXIBILITY

The processes used by a coach, a counselor, a psychotherapist or a guru are similar: they build the awareness and responsibility of the client

If you get anything at all out of this book, let it be AWARENESS and RESPONSIBILITY, not G R O W. Having said that, the strongest case for following the G R O W sequence with effective coaching questions is that it works.

It is, however, subject to recycling. What I mean by this is that one may only be able to define a vague GOAL until one has examined the REALITY in some detail. It will then be necessary to go back and define the GOAL much more precisely before moving forward again. Even a sharply defined initial GOAL may be recognized to be wrong or inappropriate once the REALITY is clear.

When listing the OPTIONS it will be necessary to check back to see if each of them would in fact move you toward the desired GOAL. Finally, before the WHAT and WHEN are set in concrete, it is crucial to make one last check to see if they meet the goal.

We will now take a deeper look at each one of these steps in turn and at the questions that best raise AWARENESS and RESPONSIBILITY within each step.

7
Goal Setting

When I want to, I perform better than when I have to.
I want to for me, I have to for you.
Self-motivation is a matter of choice.

S o much has been written about the importance and the process of goal setting that there is certainly no need for me to repeat it all in a book about coaching. Goal setting could fill a book on its own. However, I hope those who consider themselves to be goal-setting experts will forgive me if I run over those aspects of goal setting that we consider especially important for the coaching process.

We invariably begin a coaching session by determining a goal for the session itself. If the coachee has sought a session, clearly it is they who need to define what they want to get from it. Even if it is the coach or manager who has requested the session to resolve a specific issue that he spells out, the coachee can still be asked whether there is anything else they want from the session.
Questions like:

❏ What would you like to get out of this session?
❏ I have half an hour for this, where would you like to have got to by then?

THE GOAL FOR THE SESSION

❏ What would be the most helpful thing for you to take away from this session?

would elicit answers like:

❏ An outline for the month that I can develop.
❏ A clear idea of and commitment to my next two action steps.
❏ A decision as to which way to jump.
❏ An understanding of what the principal issues are.
❏ An agreed budget for the job.

THE GOAL FOR THE ISSUE

Now we come to the goal or goals related to the issue at hand, and here we need to be able to distinguish END goals from PERFORMANCE goals.

An end goal   The final objective – to become the market leader, to be appointed sales director, to land a certain key account, to win the gold medal – is seldom absolutely within your own control. You cannot know or control what your competitors will do.

A performance goal   Identify the performance level that you believe will provide you with a very good chance of achieving the end goal. It is largely within your control and it generally provides a means of measuring progress. Examples of performance goals might be for 95 percent of production to pass quality control first time, for us to sell 100 widgets next month, or to have run the mile in 4 mins 10 secs by the end of September. Importantly, it is far easier to commit yourself to, and take responsibility for, a performance goal, which is within your control, than an end goal, which is not. An end goal should wherever possible be supported by a performance goal. The end goal may provide the inspiration, but the performance goal defines the specification.

Performance goals are crucial   The lack of an established performance goal played a major role in a notorious upset for Britain in the 1968 Olympics. Welshman Lyn Davies had won the gold medal in the long jump in 1964 and he, Igor Ter-Ovanesyan, a Russian, and Ralph Boston, the American champion, were expected to share the medals. Along came a very erratic American, Bob Beamon, who, in the very first round, jumped some two feet beyond the world record. When one considers that the world record had risen by only six inches since 1936, this was a truly prodigious feat. Davies, Boston and Ter-Ovanesyan were all completely demoralized, and although Boston got the bronze and the Russian was fourth, both were six inches behind their best. Davies, who was a foot behind his best, admits he was only focused on the gold, and that if he had set himself a performance goal of, say, 27 feet, or a personal best, and kept going for that, he would have won the silver.

End and performance goals sometimes need to be topped and tailed by two other components, if not exactly goals. Take the example of Rebecca Stevens, the first British woman to climb Mount Everest. She gives lectures on her lofty achievements to businesses but also schools. You can be certain that after hearing her inspirational talk, many a schoolchild has run home and begged a parent to take them rock climbing or at least to the nearest gym with a climbing wall. 'I am going to climb Everest' may be a childlike assertion, but it is also a personal dream, a vision that ignites action. Sometimes we need to remind ourselves, or be reminded by a good question, of what inspired us to start or continue to do what we want. We could call that a dream goal.

After some considerable climbing experience, Rebecca Stevens reached the skill level from which climbing Everest seemed to be a reasonable end goal; if climbing Everest can ever be considered reasonable! However, she still had a vast amount of work, preparation training and acclimatization to do. Had she not been willing to invest herself fully in that process, Everest would have remained but a dream. 'How much are you willing to invest in the process?' is a question I often ask in the goal-setting stage of coaching for any activity. I call this the process or even the work goal.

Although company directors may be free to set their own goals, all too often they pass goals down the line as imperatives not to be questioned. This denies ownership to those who are expected to meet these targets and their performance is likely to suffer accordingly. Wise directors will strive to maintain a healthy detachment from their own goals when they are seeking to motivate their managers and will always encourage them to set their own challenging goals whenever feasible. But if they don't do this and a job is tightly proscribed, all is not totally lost, for the manager may at least be able to offer his staff some choice and ownership of how a job is done, who does what and when.

COACHING FOR OWNERSHIP

Even if a certain goal is an absolute imperative it is still possible to coach for ownership. I was recently discussing firearms training with a county police force. 'How would it be possible to have trainees own the absolute, inflexible rules of firearms safety?', they asked. I suggested that instead of presenting them with these rules at the outset, they should have a discussion, using coaching, out of which the trainees would create their own agreed set of safety rules. The chances are that it would closely parallel the institutional ones. Where they were at variance, the reasons for the variation could be coached out of the trainees, with minimal input from the tutor. This way the trainees would have a far greater degree of appreciation, understanding and ownership of the institutional firearms safety rules.

WHOSE GOAL?

The value of choice and responsibility in terms of self-motivation should never be underestimated. For example, if a sales team comes up with a goal that is lower than the boss wishes, he should consider the consequences very carefully before overriding their figure and imposing his own. He may do better to swallow his pride and accept their figure. Insisting on his may well have the effect of lowering the performance of the team even though his target was higher than theirs. They may or may not consider his figure discouragingly unrealistic, but they will certainly be demotivated by their lack of choice. Of course, the boss has one more option if he is sure of his ground and that is to start with the team's figure and coach them upwards by exploring and helping them to dismantle their barriers to achieving more. They then retain responsibility for the finally agreed figure.

In addition to supporting an end goal, which is not in your control, with a performance goal, which is, goals need to be not only S M A R T:

QUALITIES OF A GOOD GOAL

❏ Specific
❏ Measurable
❏ Agreed
❏ Realistic
❏ Time phased

but P U R E:

❏ Positively stated
❏ Understood
❏ Relevant
❏ Ethical

and C L E A R:

❏ Challenging
❏ Legal
❏ Environmentally sound
❏ Appropriate
❏ Recorded

The point of a goal having most of these qualities is self-evident and needs no further elaboration, but a couple of observations may be in order.

If a goal is not REALISTIC, there is no hope, but if it is not CHALLENGING, there is no motivation. So there is an envelope here into which all goals should fit.

It is very important to state goals in the POSITIVE. What happens if a goal is stated in the negative, for example 'We must not remain at the bottom of the regional sales league'? What is the attention focused on? Being at the bottom of the league, of course! If I say to you, 'Don't think about a red balloon', what comes to mind? Or if I say to a child, 'Don't drop that glass, spill the water, make a mistake'? The example I like is from cricket, when a wicket falls and, just as the next batsman passes through the white picket fence, some wag says to him, 'Don't get out first ball.' He has the whole long walk to the crease to think about getting out first ball, and so he does. Negative goals can easily be converted into the positive opposite, for example 'We are going for fourth in the league or higher' or 'I am going to block the first ball however tempting it may be.'

We tend to get what we focus on. If we fear failure, we are focused on failure and that is what we get

Goals must be AGREED between all the parties involved: the boss who thinks he ought to set them, the sales manager and the team who have to do the job. Without agreement, the vital ownership and responsibility of the sales team is lost, and their performance will suffer accordingly.

Coaching aims to eliminate both the external and the internal obstacles to achievement of a goal

It may appear preachy to suggest that goals should be LEGAL, ETHICAL and ENVIRONMENTALLY SOUND, but each individual has their own personal code about these things and the only way to ensure employees' full alignment is to conform to the highest standards. Younger employees today tend to have higher ethical standards than their older managers, who are often surprised and whose excuse is the usual 'we have always done it that way'. Besides, the new accent on accountability in business and throughout society, and the consequences of exposure by a whistle-blower or a consumer watchdog, surely outweigh any short-term gain that may tempt the unscrupulous! In *Sporting Excellence* David Hemery quotes Sir Michael Edwardes as saying:

You will not get the TOP people working with you unless you have the highest standards of business integrity. If you value what you get out of corner cutting at £1000, the damage you do in demotivation of good people is minus £20,000.

Some effort may need to be made to ensure that all goals are clearly UNDERSTOOD, for all too often inaccurate assumptions may distort some people's perception, even of goals they have been a party to creating.

Perhaps the most striking example of good and successful goal setting I know also comes from the Olympics. An American college freshman called John Nabor watched Mark Spitz win an extraordinary seven gold medals for swimming in the 1972 Olympics in Munich. There and then John decided that he would win the gold in the 100 meters backstroke in 1976. Although he had won the National Junior Championship at the time, he was still nearly five seconds off the pace required to win the Olympics – a huge amount to make up at that age and over such a short distance.

He decided to make the impossible possible first by setting himself a performance goal of a new world record, and then by dividing his five-second deficit by the number of hours' training he could muster in four years. He worked out that he had to improve his time by one fifth of an eyeblink for every hour of training and he felt that was possible if he worked intelligently as well as hard. It was.

He had improved so much by 1976 that he was made captain of the American swimming team for Montreal and he won the gold in both the 100 meters and the 200 meters backstroke, the first in world record time and the second as an Olympic record. Good goal setting! John Nabor was motivated by a clearly defined END goal, which he supported by a PERFORMANCE goal that was within his control. He underpinned this with a systematic PROCESS and this formed the dais on which he was to stand.

OLYMPIC GOAL

Those who have to win, win a lot Those who fear losing, lose a lot

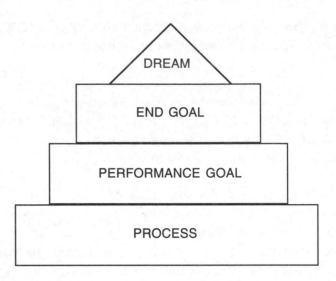

Throughout the four chapters covering each segment of the coaching sequence I will illustrate the points made with the dialogue of a fictional coaching session with Joe Butter. Joe is a senior accounts manager in a London advertising agency. His early meteoric rise through the ranks has slowed in the last two years, coinciding with the onset of middle age and the increase in his intake of food and drink, resulting in the expansion of his girth. Recently he tried to cut back and began taking exercise, but he was plagued by boredom, failure, excuses, guilt and lack of commitment. He shares his concern with a colleague, Mike, who offers to coach him on it.

MIKE   Okay, Joe, what would you like to have by the end of this half-hour?

JOE   Some kind of plan to get fitter.

MIKE   For the rest of your life or what?

JOE   No, that would be too tall an order, and besides it

might change once I get going. A realistic program for three months would be great.

MIKE   Let's look long term for a moment. What is the purpose of getting fitter for you?

JOE   I'm just feeling lousy about myself, and my work is suffering. I want to feel good again.

MIKE   Fine. How fit would you like to be by when?

JOE   I would like to lose 15 pounds or so, and within a few months be able not only to run upstairs and for the train without getting out of breath, but actually to enjoy running.

MIKE   Exactly what weight do you want to get down to, and by what date?

JOE   210 pounds by the end of the summer; that's about 15 pounds I have to lose.

MIKE   What day exactly?

JOE   20 September.

MIKE   Today is 19 February, so that gives you seven months.

JOE   Hmm! Two pounds a month, or maybe it will go faster to begin with.

MIKE   What do you want to lose by 1 June?

JOE   Ten pounds by then.

MIKE   You could do that by not eating and yet not be much fitter. How can we measure fitness?

JOE   I'll run 20 miles a week from the beginning of September onwards.

MIKE   Any particular speed?

JOE   No, I'll be happy to do it at all, and I'll know if I'm doing it satisfactorily.

MIKE   I don't care what speed, Joe, just give yourself a target speed. What will it be?

JOE   OK, nine-minute miles.

Joe now has a goal for the session, a long-term goal and a half-way mark. His goals are specific, measurable and probably incorporate all the qualities we recommend. Because there are no corporate imperatives in this case, he has complete and total responsibility for his own goals. Now it is time to take a look at REALITY.

8
What Is Reality?

*H*aving defined various goals, we need to clarify the current situation. It can be argued that goals cannot be established until the current situation is known and understood, and that we should begin with REALITY. I reject this argument on the basis that a purpose is essential to give value and direction to any discussion. Even if goals can be only loosely defined before the situation is looked at in some detail, this needs to be done first. Then, when the reality is clear, the goals can be brought into sharper focus or even altered if the situation turns out to be a little different from what was previously thought.

BE OBJECTIVE

The most important criterion for examining REALITY is objectivity. Objectivity is subject to major distortions caused by the opinions, judgments, expectations, prejudices, concerns, hopes and fears of the perceiver. Awareness is perceiving things as they really are; self-awareness is recognizing those internal factors that distort one's own perception of reality. Most people think that they are objective, but absolute objectivity does not exist. The best we have is a degree of it, but the closer we manage to get to it the better.

DETACHMENT

To approach REALITY, then, the potential distortions of both the coach and the coachee must be bypassed. This demands a high degree of detachment on the part of the coach, and the ability to phrase questions in a way that demands factual answers of the coachee. 'What were the factors that determined your decision?' will evoke a more accurate response than 'Why did you do that?', which tends to produce what the coachee believes the coach wishes to hear, or a defensive justification.

DESCRIPTION, NOT JUDGMENT

The coach should use, and as far as possible encourage the coachee to use, descriptive terminology rather than evaluative terminology. This helps to maintain detachment and objectivity and reduces the counter-productive self-criticism that distorts perception. The diagram that follows perhaps best illustrates the point.

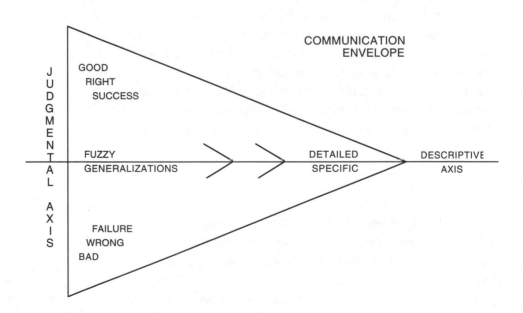

The terminology used in normal conversation, and many managerial interactions, falls generally toward the left-hand end. In coaching we try to move to the right. The more specific and descriptive our words and phrases become, the less criticism they tend to carry, and the more productive the coaching will be.

Care should be taken to remain close to the horizontal axis as often as possible. After all, there is not much I can do with the knowledge that my presentation was bad, but if I receive feedback that it was clearly structured, monotonic, brief, colorfully illustrated and beneath the knowledge level of the audience, I am in a much better position to make improvements. Of course, some words such as colors or dimensions are purely descriptive; others acquire a vertical value only when some ideal is agreed. Yet others contain within them a degree of value in most usage (words such as lively or weak); but some are essentially evaluative, like good and bad or right and wrong. So, don't just tell a marksman that he missed – that will only make him feel bad. He wants to know that his shot was three centimeters above the bull and one and a half to the right if he is to make the correction. Description adds value, criticism usually detracts.

REALITY questions, when applied to self, provide the most straightforward means of self-assessment. More about this and the way it can be applied for self-development is given in Chapter 17, but the skill of asking effective REALITY questions is paramount whatever the application.

DEEPER AWARENESS

If a coach only asks questions and receives answers from the normal level of conscious awareness, he may be helping the coachee to structure their thoughts, but he is not probing to new or deeper levels of awareness. When the coachee has to stop to think before responding, maybe raising his eyes to do so, awareness is being raised. The coachee is having to plumb new depths of his consciousness to retrieve the information. It is as if he is delving into his inner filing cabinet to find the answer. Once found, this new awareness becomes conscious, and the coachee is empowered by it.

We have a measure of choice and control over what we are aware of, but what we are unaware of controls us.

FOLLOW THE COACHEE

The good coach will be inclined to follow the interest or chain of thought of the coachee, while at the same time monitoring how that relates to the subject as a whole. Only when the coachee is ready to leave each aspect of the issue should the coach raise anything that he deems to have been omitted. If the coachee seems to have wandered far off the track, a question like 'In what way does this relate to the problem?' may bring him back or reveal a valid reason. Either way it allows him to continue to lead the process.

By following the coachee's train of thought, rather than asserting his own, the coach gains the coachee's confidence, because the latter's interest and need are being respected. For example, in the business context, say a senior manager, Alison, wants to investigate and correct an apparent problem in Peter's department. If she raises the problem at the outset, he is liable to feel threatened and become defensive. If that happens, his description of what has occurred will be distorted to make things look better than they are. However, if she lets him lead the conversation, will it ever arrive at the matter she wishes to address? Perhaps not initially, but if Alison bides her time, or more commonly bites her tongue, Peter may begin to feel safe enough to raise the matter himself. He will seldom have no idea that a problem exists, though at first he may not want to admit it to himself or others. When a subordinate begins to see his manager as a support rather than a threat, he will be much happier to raise his problems. When this happens, honest diagnosis and dialog are possible, leading to early resolution.

The blame culture that still prevails in the majority of businesses works against this, as it causes 'false reality syndrome' or 'I will tell you what I think you want to hear, or what will keep me out of trouble.' Any corrections put in place thereafter will be based on a false reality. The wise manager starts with a more general investigation and

Coaching may be requested by a coachee or a coach or it may follow a pre-planned schedule

follows the conversation of the coachee. The manager might assist the coachee with another, lesser difficulty, thereby establishing credentials as a support, rather than a threat. This approach is far more likely to lead in due course to the cause of the problem, instead of the symptom that is what is seen at first. **Problems must be addressed at the level beneath that at which they show themselves, if they are to be permanently eliminated.**

In the majority of business coaching scenarios, the REALITY will concern the facts and figures, the incidents that occurred, the actions taken, the obstacles to be overcome, the resources and people available etc. – things called up by and from the mind. However, if the coachee is learning a new physical skill, such as operating a tool of his trade, from a railway engine to a tennis racket, the coaching will also be focused on the senses: feel, sound and sight.

Body awareness brings with it automatic self-correction. If this at first seems hard to believe, just close your eyes for a moment and focus your attention internally on to your facial muscles. You will probably notice a furrowed brow or a tight jaw. Almost simultaneously with that awareness you are likely to experience a letting go, after which the brow or the jaw will be fully relaxed. The same principle applies to a complex physical movement. If attention is focused internally on the moving parts, the efficiency-reducing tensions will be felt and automatically released, resulting in improved performance. This is the basis of the new coaching approach to sporting technique and proficiency.

Internal awareness increases body efficiency, which in turn results in improved technique. It is technique from inside out rather than from outside in. Furthermore it is technique owned, integrated and unique to the body concerned, as opposed to someone else's idea of good technique to which you have forced your body to conform. Which is likely to lead to optimum performance?

USE THE SENSES

TAP THE EMOTIONS

The senses are one aspect of self-awareness. Another aspect is emotions, which have particular relevance to interpersonal problems at work or indeed elsewhere. Questions such as these will be used:

❏ What do you feel when summoned unexpectedly to the boss's office?
❏ What emotions are you left with following the recent round of redundancies?
❏ What do you think you are afraid of?
❏ Where in your body do you experience tension?
❏ In what ways do you inhibit your potential?
❏ What is the predominant feeling you have when you know you have done a good job?
❏ Can you give me a rating on a scale of one to ten for your level of confidence in your ability to give a good presentation this afternoon?

ASSESS THE ATTITUDES

Self-awareness also needs to be brought to bear on our thoughts and attitudes in the moment, and on those to which we normally have less conscious access. Each of us brings with us, sometimes right from our childhood, long-standing beliefs and opinions that will color our perceptions and our relationships with others. If we fail to acknowledge their existence and to compensate for their effects, our sense of REALITY will be distorted by them.

The interconnectedness of body and mind Most thoughts carry an emotion with them; all emotions are reflected in the body; bodily sensations often trigger thoughts. It follows therefore that concerns, blockages and inhibitions can be approached through the mind, the body or the emotions, and a clearing of one tends to free the others, although not always. Persistent stress, for example, may be reduced by identifying bodily tensions; by evoking awareness of the feelings that fuel overwork; by uncovering mental attitudes such as perfectionism. It may be necessary to work on all three separately.

Here I remind you of Timothy Gallwey's theme that the player of the Inner Game improves performance by seeking

Trying hard or trying to change causes bodily tension and uncoordinated action, which all too often results in failure

to remove or reduce the inner obstacles to outer performance.

It is time for a word of caution. A coach may become aware of probing deeper into a coachee's hidden drives and motives than anticipated. That is the nature of coaching: it addresses cause, not merely symptom. Coaching may be more demanding than papering over the interpersonal cracks in the office with directives, but it is also more rewarding in terms of results. However, if you are inadequately trained in coaching or faint hearted, stay out! If you suspect that a staff relationship problem has deep-seated origins, then it is better to bring in a professional with the necessary skills. One distinction between coaching and counseling is that coaching is mainly proactive and counseling is generally reactive. Another is that coaching generally addresses issues directly related to the workplace, but counseling skills are needed if the issue is ongoing or has childhood origins.

LIMIT THE DEPTH

REALITY QUESTIONS

The reality questions especially need to follow the 'watch the ball' guidelines discussed earlier. Here they are repeated in slightly different terms. They are as follows:

❑ The demand for an answer is essential to **compel the coachee to think**, to examine, to look, to feel, to be engaged.
❑ The questions need to demand **high resolution focus** to obtain the detail of high-quality input.
❑ The reality answers sought should be **descriptive not judgmental**, to ensure honesty and accuracy.
❑ The answers must be of sufficient quality and frequency to provide the coach with a **feedback loop**.

It is in this REALITY phase of coaching that questions should most often be initiated by the interrogatives WHAT, WHEN,

WHERE, WHO and HOW MUCH. HOW and WHY should be used only sparingly or when no other phrase will suffice. These two words invite analysis and opinion, as well as defensiveness, whereas the interrogatives seek facts. In the REALITY phase of coaching facts are important and, as in police investigation, analysis before all the facts are in can lead to theory formation and biased data collection thereafter. Coaches will need to be especially alert, listening and watching to pick up all the clues that indicate the direction of questioning to be followed. It must be stressed here that it is the coachee whose awareness is being raised. The coach often does not need to know the whole history of a situation, but merely to be certain that the coachee is clear about it. This is therefore not as time consuming as it would be were the coach to need all the facts in order to provide the best answer.

One REALITY question that seldom fails to contribute value is 'What action have you taken on this so far?' followed by 'What were the effects of that action?' This serves to emphasize the value of action, and the difference between action and thinking about problems. Often people have thought about problems for ages, but only when asked what they have done about them do they realize that they have actually taken no action at all.

EARLY RESOLUTION

It is surprising how often the thorough investigation of REALITY throws up the answer before one even enters the third and fourth stages of coaching. Obvious courses of action that emerge in the REALITY or even on occasion the GOAL stage are often accompanied by a 'Eureka!' cry of recognition and an extra impulse to complete the task. The value of this is such that coaches should be willing to dwell sufficiently long in GOALS and REALITY and resist the temptation to rush on into OPTIONS prematurely. So, lest we do just that, let us revisit the coaching session that Mike is giving Joe.

MIKE   So much for your goals, Joe; now let's have a look at things as they stand now. How much do you weigh?

JOE   225 pounds in my clothes.

MIKE   When did you last weigh yourself?

JOE   Last week sometime.

MIKE   Next door in the bathroom are some scales. Would you hop on them now?

JOE   … Oh sugar! I'm 235 pounds.

MIKE   Do you eat excessively?

JOE   Yes, I'm a bit of a chocoholic and I do like rich food.

MIKE   Have you been eating a lot recently?

JOE   More than usual. I seem to when I am worried.

MIKE   What are you worried about now?

JOE   My health, middle age and I feel a bit insecure about my job right now.

MIKE   Which bothers you most?

JOE   My health, I suppose, because I'm convinced that if I could get a grip on that, my state of mind and therefore my work would improve.

MIKE   OK, let's stay with that for today, but in another session we could look specifically at your state of mind or your work. What do you eat too much of?

JOE   Chips and desserts.

MIKE   At every meal?

JOE   Most days both at least once.

MIKE   At home or when you're out? Lunch or in the evenings?

JOE   In the evenings at home, and when we eat out at least two evenings a week.

MIKE   With friends or with your wife?

JOE   Mainly just the two of us.

MIKE   Does your wife like to eat a lot too?

JOE   Not really, but she knows I enjoy it so she goes along with it.

MIKE   So you like sweets and chips, eat more when you are worried, and this is generally in the evenings and with the family. What about drink?

JOE   I sometimes have a beer at lunchtime, and I usually have a bottle of plonk in the evening.

MIKE   Exactly how many beers have you had in the last seven days?

JOE   Let me see … about 12.

MIKE   And the week before?

JOE   About the same, if I'm honest.

MIKE   Shall we look at exercise now?

JOE   OK. I have started running, at least.

MIKE   How often do you run and for how long?

JOE   I do about 15 minutes maybe twice a week.

MIKE   When did you run this week?

JOE   I didn't, I just felt too miserable.

MIKE   The week before?

JOE   On Sunday morning, just the once. I was going to again but my calves still hurt.

MIKE   Does the discomfort of running put you off?

JOE   Yes. Ankles, calves, thighs, heaving breath – I hate it.

MIKE   What other exercise do you take – walk, cycle, even run upstairs instead of taking the elevator?

JOE   No, but I do take an occasional sauna.

MIKE   How much do you think that helps?

JOE   It helps my guilt and it is not too strenuous.

Joe is now more honest with himself about the REALITY of his overindulgence in food and drink and of how minimal his exercise is. His wishful thinking or self-delusion is now grounded in REALITY. More importantly, he knows exactly where he is starting from.

Mike then takes him back to review his goal of 210 pounds, which is perhaps unrealistic in view of the fact that he actually weighs 235 pounds. However, Joe is so disgusted with the REALITY of his weight that he does not wish to alter the 210 pound target, even though this now requires a reduction of more than three pounds a month, average. Mike still considers it to be realistic.

Fortunately Mike offers to coach Joe on his running to try

to reduce the discomfort he experiences, so this will give us the opportunity to hear an example of coaching a physical skill. They set out on a short run together, having agreed an easy pace and a goal of finding a comfortable running style, pace and mental activity.

MIKE   OK, let's just find an initial speed that feels relatively comfortable … What are you noticing in your body?

JOE   My calves feel stiff.

MIKE   Just place all your attention on your calves and tell me exactly what you feel in them?

JOE   A tightness down the back of them.

MIKE   When do you feel it? All the time in both calves or what?

JOE   No, just when I push off, and it is more on my right than on my left.

MIKE   Give your right calf a tightness rating on a scale of one to ten, with ten being as tight as you can imagine.

JOE   Actually it's now less, but it's about a five and the left leg is a three.

MIKE   What is it now?

JOE   It's down to a three.

MIKE   Keep monitoring it and tell me when it reaches two.

JOE   Both calves are a two now or even less. They feel great, but I notice my arms hurt as I swing them.

MIKE   OK, just pay attention to the hurt in your arms and tell me more about it.

JOE   Hey, as soon as I started to pay attention to them I felt them relax, and I notice that I'm now holding them in a lower position.

MIKE   Is that more comfortable, then?

JOE   Yes, it certainly is.

MIKE   It actually looks more fluid as well.

JOE   Yes, I really feel I'm moving quite well. Normally by this point my breath is heaving, but I notice that I'm breathing quite rhythmically.

MIKE   Just follow your breathing for a while. Don't try to breathe differently, but notice the inbreath and the outbreath as it happens each time.

JOE   It's slowing down even more. I'll become a runner yet!

MIKE   What is the quality you would most like to find in your running?

JOE   You mentioned it and I'm beginning to feel it – flowing.

MIKE   OK, just rate how much you're flowing on a 1–10 scale.

JOE   Well, it was about four but it's already a six.

MIKE   Where in your body do you take your reading from?

JOE   My shoulders, funnily enough.

MIKE   What is it now?

JOE   It's an eight! I feel great!

MIKE Yes, and we're back at base three minutes faster than you thought you could do it.

JOE   That's amazing. I feel I could do another 15 minutes, no sweat.

MIKE You will before long. Well done. You see how focusing the attention internally clears up problem areas, leads to relaxation, and is so interesting that boredom is eliminated. It turns a chore into a pleasure.

JOE   You never even told me how to run more efficiently, but I seem to have found that flow for myself. That makes me feel good, and opens up possibilities in other areas too.

In coaching purely to learn or develop a physical skill on the field or in real time, the process we use, repeated in different forms of course, is complete at the end of this phase. The performance improvement takes place through the application of AWARENESS during this REALITY phase, as it did for Joe. However, for the overall improvement of Joe's health and well-being, and for the furtherance of most business issues, which require planning, investigation, reviewing and the like, there are two more phases to go.

9

What Options Do You Have?

When you are sure that you have no more ideas, just come up with one more.

The purpose of the OPTIONS stage is not to find the 'right' answer but to create and list as many alternative courses of action as possible. The quantity of options is more important at this stage than the quality and feasibility of each one. The brain-stimulating process of gathering all the options is as valuable as the option list itself, because it gets the creative juices flowing. It is from this broad base of creative possibilities that specific action steps will be selected. If preferences, censorship, ridicule, obstacles or the need for completeness are expressed during the collection process, potentially valuable contributions will be missed and the choices will be limited.

MAXIMIZING CHOICES

The coach will do all he can to draw these options from the coachee or from the team he is coaching/managing. To do this he needs to create an environment in which participants will feel safe enough to express their thoughts and ideas without inhibition or fear of judgment from the coach or others. All contributions, however apparently silly, need to be noted down, usually by the coach, in case they contain a germ of an idea that may leap into significance in the light of later suggestions.

NEGATIVE ASSUMPTIONS

One of the factors that most restricts the generation of creative solutions to business and other issues is the implicit assumptions we carry, many of which we are barely conscious of. For example:

❏ It can't be done.
❏ It can't be done like that.
❏ They would never agree to that.
❏ It's bound to cost too much.
❏ We can't afford the time.
❏ The competition must have thought of that.

There are many more. Note that all of them contain a negative or a dismissal. A good coach would invite his coachees to ask themselves 'What if…' For example:

❏ What if you had a large enough budget?
❏ What if you had more staff?
❏ What if you knew the answer? What would it be?
❏ What if that obstacle did not exist? What would you do then?

By this process, which temporarily sidesteps the censorship of the rational mind, more creative thought is unleashed and perhaps the obstacle is found to be less insurmountable than it had always seemed. Perhaps another team member might know a way round that particular obstacle, so the impossible is made possible by the combined contributions of more than one person.

THE NINE DOT EXERCISE

On our training courses for coaches we use the well-known nine dot exercise to illustrate graphically the self-limiting assumptions we all tend to make. For those of you who are not familiar with the exercise, or who have done it but may not remember the answer, here it is.

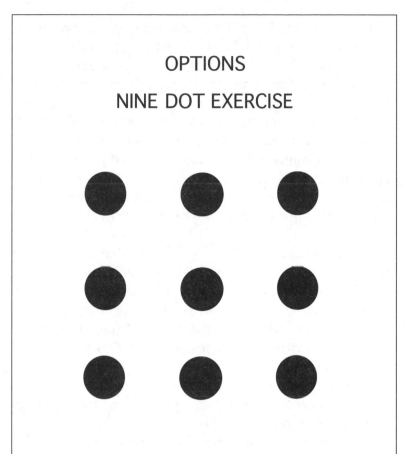

OPTIONS

NINE DOT EXERCISE

Join the nine dots, using four straight lines only. Your pen must not leave the page and you may not repeat any line.

You may have remembered or realized that the assumption that has to be eliminated is the one that says, 'You have to stay within the square'. However, don't become too smug. Can you do it again with the same rules but using three lines or less? What assumptions are you limiting yourself with now?

Of course, no one said you had to draw your line through the middle of the dots, but I bet you assumed that. What about two lines, or even one?

No one said you could not tear the page out and roll it into a cone, tear it into three strips, or fold it like a concertina. What this has done is to break another assumption, the one that thought we only had one variable, the position of the lines. But who said you could not move the dots? Recognizing all the available variables will expand our thinking and our list of options. Breaking out of these self-limiting assumptions frees us to solve old problems in new ways. The key is to identify the false assumption; the resolution is then much more easy to find. (Several nine-dot solutions are on page 177.)

SORTING OPTIONS

Benefits and costs   Once a comprehensive list has been generated, the WILL phase of coaching may just be a simple matter of selecting the best of the bunch. However, in more complex issues, as so many in business are, it may be necessary to reexamine the list by noting the benefits and costs of each of the courses of action. This should again be done by coaching, and it is here that some blend of two or more ideas may emerge as the optimum. Here I sometimes invite the coachee to note how much he likes each option on the list on a 1–10 scale.

Input from the coach   What does the coach do if he has particular knowledge, skill or experience of the matter in question and the coachee has not come up with what is, to the coach, the obvious solution? At what stage should the coach offer his expertise? Clearly, when he recognizes that the coachee has exhausted his possibilities. But how can he provide his input and still not undermine the coachee's sense of total ownership? Quite simply by saying, 'I have another couple of possible options. Would you like to have them?' Very few coachees will ever say no, but they might ask the coach to wait while they complete a particular train of thought. Any suggestions provided by the coach should only be accorded the same importance as all the other OPTIONS.

Mapping the options In the listing of OPTIONS, the subconscious hierarchy (the more important things come first) that exists when a vertical column is made can be avoided by writing them randomly on a paper in the way a crossword expert solves an anagram.

Let us see how Mike, who happens to be a bit of a fitness buff himself, tackles the OPTIONS issue with JOE, who clearly expects some prescription from the expert for his unhealthy condition.

MIKE   So what are all the different things you could do, Joe, to get yourself leaner and fitter?

JOE   I could run more often, or further or faster.

MIKE   What else?

JOE   I could cut down my eating, and my drinking.

MIKE   What else?

JOE   I could eat fewer fatty foods.

MIKE   What other forms of exercise could you take?

JOE   Oh well, I suppose I could go to the gym.

MIKE   Anything else?

JOE   I could swim or I could even take up squash, which is something I've thought about at times. Or golf.

MIKE   What else could you do that requires no investment, no equipment, no clubs to join, just within your normal life?

JOE   I can't think of anything. I couldn't cycle, because I don't have a bike and I'm not going to buy one for that!

MIKE   What if you did have one?

JOE   I could cycle to work – and to the pub! I could actually walk to work and run up the stairs rather than take the lift to the fourth floor.

MIKE   Indeed you could. Is that it?

JOE   That's enough, isn't it?

MIKE   Would you like one more option to consider?

JOE   Sure, if you have one.

MIKE   How about weights and an exercise regime at home?

JOE   Yes, that's possible too.

Joe and Mike then examine the list and consider the advantages and disadvantages of these options. Golf is time consuming. Squash is a much quicker and more strenuous form of exercise, but it takes a little time to learn to get the best out of it. The nearest swimming pool is five miles away, but swimming is injury free. Together they explore the practicalities of certain diets and of being able to stay off drink in the business environment.

FIT FOR WORK

Lest you are thinking that this example of coaching is a little removed from the business context, you might consider the following statement made by Sir Michael Edwardes in an interview with David Hemery for his book *Sporting Excellence*:

I am always very hesitant about bringing an unfit, overweight person into a team; it suggests a lack of discipline. I am sixty and play squash three times a week and tennis once. I'm not overweight. My energy is greater than it was at fifty. I'm sure I'm fitter than my opposition and I think that is material. I wouldn't want anyone on my team who wasn't physically fit.

Joe is now aware of all the OPTIONS and is pretty clear about their various pros and cons. Decision time has arrived.

10
What Will You Do?

Decision time and time for precision.

T he purpose of this final phase of the coaching sequence is to convert a discussion into a decision. It is the construction of an action plan to meet a requirement that has been clearly specified, on ground that has been thoroughly surveyed, and using the widest possible choice of building materials.

The following set of WILL questions are applicable to the majority of coaching situations. Of course, the coach will add subsets of questions to clarify each of these points, but the principal questions form an effective backbone for this phase.

The demands of a managerial autocrat are often met with quiet resignation, resistance or resentment, however diplomatically they are expressed. A coach, on the other hand, can bring a surprising degree of toughness into this phase of his questioning without causing any bad feelings, since he is not imposing his own will but activating the will of the coachee. The coachee always maintains choice and ownership, even if their decision is to take no action, and therefore they will not feel oppressed by hard questions. They might even be amused by the recognition of their own ambivalence. If they do feel pushed, it suggests that the coach is unconsciously revealing that he thinks the coachee *should* take a particular action.

I will now look at the value, the objective and the best way to ask each of these questions.

What are you going to do?   This question is quite distinct from 'What could you do?' or 'What are you thinking of doing?' or 'Which of these do you prefer?'. None of these implies a firm decision. Once the coach has asked this question in a clear, firm voice, indicating that it is decision time, he may follow it up with a question like 'Which of these alternatives are you going to act on?' In most coaching issues the action plan will incorporate more than one of the options or parts of the options combined.

The options have been only loosely defined. Now is the time for the coach to ask questions to clarify the detail of the chosen options. By far the most important of these will be:

When are you going to do it?   This is the toughest of all the questions. We all have big ideas of what we would like to do or are going to do, but it is only when we time frame it that it takes on a level of reality. And sometime next year is insufficient too. If something is going to happen the timing needs to be highly specific.

If a single action is required the answer sought might be 'at 10.00 a.m. next Tuesday, the 12th'. Often both a starting time and date and a finishing date will be required. If the action to be followed is a repetitive one, then the intervals need to be specified: 'We will meet at 9.00 a.m. on the first Wednesday of every month.' It is up to the coach to tie the coachee down to exact timings. The coachee may wriggle but a good coach will not let him off the hook.

Will this action meet your goal?   Now that we have an action and a time frame, it is important before we proceed any further to check that this is leading in the direction of both the goal of the session and the long-term goal. Without checking back the coachee may find that he has wandered a long way off track. If this has happened, it is important not to rush to change the action, but to check if in fact it is the goal that needs to be modified in the light of what has come up since it was defined.

What obstacles might you meet along the way? It is important to prepare for and preempt any circumstances that could arise that would inhibit completion of the action. Disruptive external scenarios might be looming, but internal ones could also occur, such as the faint-heartedness of the coachee. Some people experience a shrinking commitment and just can't wait for an obstacle to appear and provide them with an excuse for non-completion. This can be preempted by the coaching process.

Who needs to know? All too frequently in business, plans are changed and the people who should be told promptly hear this only later and at second hand, something that is very bad for staff relations. The coach needs to satisfy himself that all the appropriate people are listed and that a plan is made for them to be informed.

What support do you need? This is possibly related to the previous question, but support can come in many different forms. It could mean an arrangement to bring in outside people, skills or resources, or it could be as simple as informing a colleague of your intention and asking them to remind you or keep you on target. Merely sharing your intended action with another person often has the effect of ensuring that you do it.

How and when are you going to get that support? It is no good wanting some support but not taking the steps necessary to get it. Here the coach needs to persist until the coachee's actions are clear and certain.

What other considerations do you have? This is a necessary catch-all question so that the coachee cannot claim that the coach omitted something. It is the coachee's responsibility to ensure that nothing is left out.

Rate on a 1-10 scale the degree of certainty you have that you will carry out the actions agreed This is not rating the certainty of the outcome actually happening. It is a rating of the coachee's intention to carry out his part of the job. Completion of the task may depend on the agreement or the actions of others, and that cannot be rated.

What prevents it from being a 10? If you have rated yourself at less than eight, how can you reduce the size of the task or lengthen the time scale such that it would enable you to raise the rating to eight or above? If your rating is still below eight, cross out the action step, as you are unlikely to take it.

COMPLETION

This is not to sabotage completion, as it might appear, but it is our experience that those who rate at less than eight seldom follow through. However, when faced with having to admit failure, the coachee may all of a sudden find the necessary motivation.

Most of us are familiar with the items that keep recurring on our job lists, be it at work or just the odd jobs around the home. Our list becomes so crumpled and scribbled on that eventually we rewrite it, and those same few items keep getting copied over. In time we begin to feel appropriately guilty but still nothing happens. 'How is it that I never complete this?' we moan at ourselves. Our incompleted job list is evidence of our failure. Well, why feel bad about it? If you are not going to do something, cross it off your list. And if you want to be a success for ever more, don't put anything on your list that you don't intend to do!

Remember that coaching aims to build and maintain the self-belief of the coachee. We must therefore coach people to success for their own sake as well as for their company.

CONCLUDING THE COACHING CYCLE

At this point the coaching cycle is complete, but it is up to the coach to hand to the coachee a clear and accurate written record of the action steps agreed and the coachee's answers to all the WILL questions. He should get the coachee to read it and confirm that it is a true record, that it constitutes his plan, that he fully understands it, and that he intends to carry it out. This is when I as coach usually offer myself as further support and reassure the coachee of my accessibility should he need me. Sometimes I offer to initiate the contact myself after a suitable interval just to see how things are going. All this serves to help the coachee realize that he matters. I want the coachee to leave the session feeling good about himself and about his chances of getting the job done. If he does, then it will be.

Let us look at how Mike handles this final and important WILL phase with Joe.

MIKE   Well, Joe, we have a list here. Let me remind you:

> Running more often, further or faster.
> Eating and drinking less and more healthily.
> Visiting a gym.
> Swimming.
> Squash.
> Golf.
> Cycling.
> Walking.
> Running upstairs.
> Weights and/or exercises at home.

Which of these are you going to do?

JOE   I am definitely going to continue running, with a minimum of three times a week for 20 minutes.

MIKE   When are you going to start that?

JOE   Next week, with the first run on Tuesday.

MIKE   Which day and what time each day are you going to run?

JOE   Usually Tuesday and Thursday immediately I get home from work, and on Sunday mornings. Sunday I'll do half an hour.

MIKE   What else are you going to do?

JOE   I'm going to cut out chips and chocolate altogether.

MIKE   What about drink?

JOE   I was hoping you wouldn't ask that one directly! But yes, no more wine and only half a pint of beer a day.

MIKE   How realistic is that? Can you stick to a half-pint if you are with friends?

JOE   Probably not.

MIKE   I have a suggestion.

JOE   What?

MIKE   Three and a half pints a week. If you OD one day you just hold off the next one or two to make good.

JOE   Sounds good – much easier to stick to but with the same result.

MIKE   When do you start?

JOE   Sunday.

MIKE   What other exercise?

JOE   I'll arrange for a couple of squash lessons to see if I like it and can get started.

MIKE   When?

JOE   I knew you were going to ask that! I'll call the pro today and have my first lesson next week.

MIKE   And the next lesson?

JOE   The next week.

MIKE   What else?

JOE   Well, I'm certainly not going to start cycling to work in November. I'll put that on the shelf for reconsideration on 1 April.

MIKE   I'll remind you [*taking out his diary*] and I'm not fooling either!

JOE   Perhaps I could do a few exercises at home meanwhile.

MIKE   What exercises, how often?

JOE   You're the expert, you tell me.

MIKE   We'll come back to that one. Is that it?

JOE   That should be more than enough to meet my goal.

MIKE   I agree, but is it realistic?

JOE   I think so.

MIKE   Now, what obstacles can you foresee?

JOE   Christmas for the food and drink, and extreme weather for the running. That's all. Oh, and my natural laziness.

MIKE   How will you cope with those?

JOE   Give myself an extra couple of pints that week and a plate of chips! I'm on holiday the week after Christmas and I'll do two extra runs.

MIKE   What if there's bad frost or snow then or at any other time?

JOE   I'll replace the running with either squash or a swim. I know what you're going to ask. Forty minutes of squash or twenty lengths of the pool.

MIKE   What about this laziness of yours, which we all have?

JOE   I need a prod every now and again.

MIKE   Just what I was coming to. What support do you need and from whom?

JOE   My wife over the food and to prompt me to run. I'll speak to her about all this tonight.

MIKE   Any other support?

JOE   From you, a phone call every couple of weeks would help, and I'd like you to show me a couple of good exercises at home. I don't want to go and buy weights and all that.

MIKE   Sure, sit-ups like this don't demand someone to hold your feet and are just as good for the stomach muscles. Start with ten and build up your repeats. Squats like this, and push-ups. Again, groups of repetitions are better than forcing. About ten minutes each day would be great.

JOE   OK, each morning when I get up, and if I miss one day I've got a second chance in the evening. If I miss a whole day, I'll do two stints the following day.

MIKE   When are you going to start this?

JOE   How about tomorrow morning?

MIKE   You've been surprisingly willing to set yourself a fairly ambitious program, given your past history. How would you rate your chances of sticking to it for the next three months on a 1-10 scale?

JOE   That is a tough one – seven, I guess.

MIKE   What part of this could you drop or reduce so you could give yourself a higher rating?

JOE   I think it's just too much, and I'm doubtful about the squash because I won't be able to do that on my own in my own time and at short notice. If I drop that, I'll give myself a nine.

MIKE   Good. One final check, will this regime meet your goal?

JOE   It has altered its emphasis, but I think it exceeds it and I'm very confident I'll succeed.

Not all coaching sessions are as straightforward as this one, and coachees can offer more resistance and complications, but this is fairly typical and it serves to illustrate the majority of the coaching principles.

And as I have said before, most coaching sessions will be less formalized and structured than this one. Most take place in a way that might not even be recognized by the uninitiated as coaching at all. They would simply think that someone was being particularly helpful and considerate of the other, and was obviously a good listener. Structured or informal, the fundamental principles of raising AWARENESS and building RESPONSIBILITY within the performer remain the key to good coaching.

11
What Is Performance?

If either the quality of a performance or learning from the experience is important, coaching is a must. If neither is, then tell – if you must.

'The execution of the functions required of one' is how my dictionary defines performance, but that sounds not unlike doing the minimum necessary to get by. That is not performance in my view; it is not what I refer to in *Coaching for Performance*.

Real performance is going beyond what is expected; it is setting one's own highest standards, invariably standards that surpass what others demand or expect. It is, of course, an expression of one's potential. This comes closer to the second meaning of performance as defined by my dictionary: 'a deed, a feat, a public exhibition of skill'. That is what I coach for.

By definition, the full expression of one's potential demands taking total responsibility or ownership. If it did not, it would not be one's own potential, it would be partly someone else's. Coaching is, therefore, the essential management style or tool for optimizing people's potential and performance. Commanding, demanding, instructing, persuading with threats, overt or covert, cannot produce sustainable optimum performance, even though they may get the job done.

We perform quite well on autopilot with our attention elsewhere, but higher performance demands fuller attention and no distractions

The question a leader or a manager has to ask himself is how well he wants the job done or how good a performance he is looking for. And does he even know what a really good performance would look like? Coaching can lead to performance beyond the expectations of the coach/manager, and beyond the dreams of the performer.

In sport, where success and failure are so clearly defined, the rules are simple, the time span is short and physical or mental discomfort is determinate, self-motivation is not hard to evoke. The tabloids would have us believe that fame and fortune are the dream of every sports performer. For some, perhaps, but the majority are shooting for less tangible goals such as identity, self-esteem, excellence and peak experience, uniquely personal rewards only experienced by the recipient.

Success in business is less glamorous, and slow to come, by comparison. Quality of life in the workplace, by virtue of the hours and years spent there, takes on a far greater importance. Few captains of industry achieve any degree of public recognition and those who do are likely to be more infamous than famous. On the other hand, business offers countless opportunities, both large and small, for personal achievement of goals that can be individually chosen to provide optimal personal growth. Unfortunately, few people manage to view their workplace as a university for self-development, or their chores as challenges. It is hardly surprising, therefore, that their performance lacks sparkle.

THE JOHNSONVILLE SAUSAGE

Let me tell you the story of Johnsonville Sausage. That was the name of a family sausage-making business in Wisconsin, which in 1980 was under the stewardship of Ralph Stayer. Stayer wrote about his company in the November/December 1990 issue of the *Harvard Business Review* under the title 'How I Learned to Let My Workers Lead', from which I will quote.

Growth, sales and profits were good at Johnsonville

Sausage, giving all the indications of a successful business, but… 'What worried me more than the competition, however, was the gap between potential and performance,' wrote Stayer. 'No one was deliberately wasting money, time, and materials; it was just that people took no responsibility for their work. They showed up in the morning, did half-heartedly what they were told to do, and then went home.'

The situation that Stayer describes is all too common, but he clearly recognized the vital role responsibility plays in bringing performance up to potential. On his own admission Stayer then 'went from authoritarian control to authoritarian abdication'. He forced responsibility on his management team and expected them to guess what he wanted. It did not work. 'The early 1980s taught me that I couldn't give responsibility. People had to expect it, want it, even demand it … To bring people to that … I had to learn to be a better coach.'

He changed his approach. The sausage makers, instead of the top management, started tasting the sausages and took charge of quality control and of making improvements to the product and its packaging. Next the shop floor raised the issue of poor-performing colleagues:

We offered to help them set performance standards and to coach them in confronting poor performers, but we insisted that since they were the production-performance experts it was up to them to deal with the situation. I bit my tongue time and time again, but they took on the responsibility for dealing with performance problems and actually fired individuals who wouldn't perform up to the standards of their teams.

Before long the Johnsonville workforce was responsible for the vast majority of functions. Terms like employee and subordinate were dropped in favor of 'members' of the organization, and managers became known as 'coordinators' or 'coaches'. This change in language set the tone of the renewed organization, in which promotion came from ability as a teacher, coach and facilitator, rather than from managing or problem solving in the traditional sense.

Stayer noticed that the workforce:

wanted to see if I practiced what I preached. From the outset I did simple things to demonstrate my sincerity. I made a sign for my desk that said THE QUESTION IS THE ANSWER, and when people came in to me with questions, I asked myself if they were questions I should answer. Invariably they weren't. Invariably people were asking me to make decisions for them. Instead of giving answers, I turned the tables and asked the questions myself, trying to make them repossess their own problems.

As time went on the 'members' were empowered to take strategic decisions, and did so successfully, and Stayer even began to see himself as a consultant to his own company.

When I began this process of change ten years ago. I looked forward to the time when it would be all over and I could get back to my real job. But I've learned that change is the real job of every effective business leader because change is about the present and the future not about the past. There is no end to change. Yet another thing I've learned is that the cause of excitement at Johnsonville Sausage is not change itself but the process used in producing change. Learning and responsibility are invigorating, and aspirations make our hearts beat.

Getting better performance from any group or individual, yourself included, means permanent change in the way you think and run your business. Change of this kind is not a single transaction but a journey, and the journey has a specific starting point [REALITY] and a clear destination [GOAL].

So to make the changes that will lead to great performance, I recommend focusing on goals, expectations, contexts, actions, and learning.

PERFORMANCE

Stayer clearly practices what he preaches. The workforce responded with performance that was exceptional, and no doubt learning and enjoyment were very high too at Johnsonville Sausage. It takes courage to initiate such radical changes in any organization, but any business leader who seeks to be assured of real performance, and perhaps survival in the uncertain future, will do well to consider big changes. But where do you start?

Coaching for performance improvement in oneself, in others and in teams is simple and straightforward provided its underlying principles are fully embraced, and the adoption of a coaching management style is where change begins. However, even managers who use coaching widely may fail if they focus exclusively on performance improvement.

LEARNING

Many businesses are beginning to recognize that they need to become learning organizations if they are going to stimulate and motivate their staff and if they are going to cope with the demand for almost continuous change. Performance, learning and enjoyment are inextricably intertwined. All three are enhanced by high awareness levels, a fundamental objective of coaching, but it is possible to focus primarily on the development of one of them quite successfully, though only for a while. When one of the three is neglected, sooner or later the other two will suffer. For example, performance cannot be sustained where there is no learning or where there is no enjoyment.

ENJOYMENT

Many professional sports performers have experienced periods of losing the enjoyment of their sport. Likewise the enjoyment of basking on a beach may fade after a day or three and we begin to seek challenges to our performance with paddle tennis or new skills to learn like scuba diving. Schools of learning that do not offer the challenges of the performing arts or sports and that frown on enjoyment are unable to maintain the high standards of learning they so urgently and exclusively seek. The very definition of performance, for coaching purposes, should include learning and enjoyment too.

12
Learning and Enjoyment

We do not have to know how to do something to be able to do it.
We learned to walk, run, ride a bike and catch a ball without instructions.

Much of this book so far has been about learning. The learning of physical skills in sport has provided a number of examples illustrating the coaching process. But the widespread use of instructional methods of teaching in sport, at work and at school is an indication of how poor general understanding remains about how we really learn. Part of the problem is that instructors, teachers and managers are concerned more about short-term gain, passing the exam or getting the job done now, than they are about learning or about the quality of performance. This is going to have to change, because results are simply not good enough to meet our needs or the competition. We have to find a better way.

Participants on our coaching courses are struck by how obvious and commonsensical the principles of coaching are, by their irrefutible logic – once we can escape from the tyranny of old, redundant thinking patterns that we have never thought to doubt or question. Many find helpful a way of looking at learning that is widely accepted in business training circles. It postulates four stages of learning:

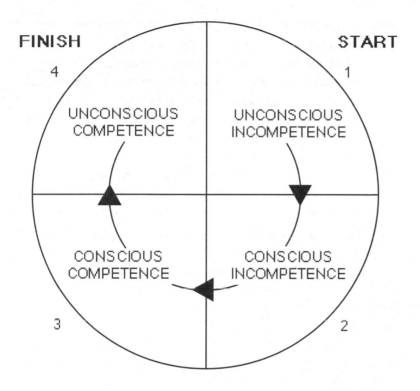

❑ **Unconscious incompetence** = low performance, no differentiation or understanding.

❑ **Conscious incompetence** = low performance, recognition of flaws and weak areas.

❑ **Conscious competence** = improved performance, conscious, somewhat contrived effort.

❑ **Unconscious competence** = natural, integrated, automatic higher performance.

The learning cycle generally takes us through each of these segments in turn. As one piece of learning becomes fully integrated, and if we are endeavoring to continue to improve, we embark on the next cycle.

Do we always have to follow these four stages, or are there exceptions or accelerations? A child learns to walk and talk, throw and catch, run and ride a bicycle by passing fairly directly from **unconscious incompetence** to **unconscious competence**. Later, when a teenager learns to drive a car, the four stages are clearly identifiable, with the driving instructor's input applied in the **conscious incompetence** and **conscious competence** stages. After the driving test, learning continues in **conscious competence** and evolves into **unconscious competence** as the act of driving becomes more integrated. Soon we are able to drive relatively automatically while concentrating on our thoughts, on a conversation or on the sounds of a CD. Driving skill continues to improve slowly by experience.

Learning can also be accelerated by consciously setting out round the cycle again. This can be done in two ways, either by employing an advanced driving instructor to take us through stages 2 and 3, or by a process of self-coaching. The first way assumes that we are incapable of determining what we are doing wrong and what we should do differently in future. We give responsibility for improvements in our driving to another person.

With the second method we retain that responsibility, shutting off the radio and our extraneous thoughts so we can observe or become aware of different aspects of our driving. If this is done consciously, non-judgmentally and honestly, those areas of our driving that need improvement will reveal themselves. It might be harsh gear changes, misjudgment of speed and distance on occasion, or tension in the arms and shoulders causing premature tiredness. We are now in the phase of **conscious incompetence**, and we are likely to enter the next phase by making a conscious effort to operate the clutch more smoothly and watch the rev counter, or watch the speedometer and always leave a set distance between our vehicle and the one in front. Eventually and by conscious repetition the improvements become a habit and **unconscious competence** commences.

There is, however, a very important variation on this theme of self-coaching that is far more effective. Instead of making the effort to change certain flawed aspects of driving that have been identified in **conscious incompetence**, we can achieve better results with less effort by doing the following.

NOT TRYING

We identify the quality we would like to bring in, say smoothness in gear changes and, rather than trying to change gear smoothly, we simply continue to observe how smooth our gear changes are. In order to quantify this to give ourselves more precise feedback measurement, we might create a 1-10 smoothness scale, with 10 representing a gear change that could not be felt at all. We would drive as normal but simply rate the smoothness to ourselves after each gear change. With no increase of effort the numbers will begin to rise, and in a surprisingly short time they are likely to hover between nine and ten.

Unconscious competence slips in, monitoring of the scale falls away, and smooth gear changes are maintained even when driving conditions become extreme or we are driving an unfamiliar vehicle. If any lapse does occur, a mere mile or two of **conscious competence** monitoring and rating will restore the smoothness. This effort-free learning or performance improvement is surprisingly fast and delivers a higher-quality result.

In process terms, this is a leap from **conscious incompetence** directly into **unconscious competence** without going through the phase of **conscious competence**. The driving instructor will keep us wallowing in **conscious incompetence** and **conscious competence**, at great expense of time and money. However, he provides the consciousness, such as it is, by his criticisms and his instructions, neither of which are owned by the learner. The more critical and dictatorial he is, the more ownership is undermined.

There is a world of difference between continuously trying to do something right and continuously monitoring what we are doing non-judgmentally. It is the latter, the input–feedback loop, that results in quality learning and performance improvement – this is allowing rather than forcing. It is the stressful former that is the least effective and the most used in common practice.

ENJOYMENT

Were I to devote an entire chapter to enjoyment in a book primarily intended for the business reader, it might cause a raised eyebrow or two. It is a subject that deserves its own chapter, but I will restrain myself! Enjoyment is experienced in many different ways by different people, but I will attempt to boil it down to an essence, in a couple of paragraphs.

Enjoyment is primarily experienced through our senses. Due to the comfortable physical security of our modern world, we are less often exposed to extreme sensations by the normal events of life at home or at work, so we invent ever more radical sports and leisure pursuits to activate our feelings. We seek ever steeper, higher, faster, tougher stimulants – but we can enjoy equally strong responses merely by enhancing our senses to experience greater subtlety. As we become more aware of our senses, ordinary, everyday sensations become literally sensational. Daily, common-or-garden events can provide intense enjoyment if we experience them more fully with all our senses.

This heightened awareness can be created in a number of ways: by deprivation or devotion, by meditation or medication, by exercise or ecstasy, but also by the simple and risk-free means of self-coaching. Asking ourselves precisely what we feel, touch, hear, see, smell, taste and even think – focusing to find the answers – heightens our awareness and our enjoyment. It gives us more and better feedback or high-quality relevant input.

Another associated form of enjoyment comes from the experience of a fuller expression of our potential. Each time we experience ourselves stretching to somewhere we have never been before in exertion, in courage, in activity, in fluidity, in dexterity, in effectiveness, we reach new heights in our senses, accentuated by the flow of adrenalin. Coaching works directly on the senses, particularly where physical activities are concerned. Therefore coaching by its very nature enhances enjoyment. In practice, the distinction between performance, learning and enjoyment

Focused attention or relaxed concentration describe the same passive receptive state

becomes blurred, and at the limit of this merger lies what is often described as the peak experience. Far be if from me to be promoting peak experiences at work, but there is a serious side to this, the need to understand the way coaching works, and awareness in particular.

Self-esteem, confidence and performance are seamless. So must be performance, learning and enjoyment – if performance is to be sustained

13
Motivation

The carrot and the stick are pervasive and persuasive motivators.
But if you treat people like donkeys, they will perform like donkeys.

The secret of motivation is the holy grail that every business leader would dearly love to find. The carrot and stick, the symbolic external motivators, are becoming less and less effective. Few managers doubt that self-motivation would be better, but forcing someone to motivate themselves is a contradiction in terms. Self-motivation dwells within the mind of each individual, out of reach of even the chiefest of executives. We know that the mind is key, but where is the key to the mind? Motivation would also appear to be easier to come by in sport than it is in business, although many sports people and their coaches are also seeking more of it. What, if anything, can we learn from sport?

The majority of sports involve the body and mind in a skill that demands balance, timing, fluidity, extension, exertion and strength in different combinations. The closer we come to using our body to the fullness of its unique potential, the more pleasure we experience from the sensations generated. Sport therefore is inherently enjoyable to the extent of being somewhat addictive; mental or physical work is far less so, at least for the majority of people. Clearly, sport has a motivational advantage here. There are other factors too.

The external rewards from sport are more immediate, more glamorous and, at the top, often richer in fortune and in fame. More importantly, however, sports performances, at all levels, ultimately are exclusively in the hands of the performers (total responsibility). Added to that, the choice to take up sport, any sport, in the first place is often driven by a desire for self-worth and identity. This constitutes a large measure of self-motivation, and now we have all the winning ingredients.

Because there is limited inherent enjoyment at work, at least for those who do not experience the responsibility advantage of working for themselves, employers have had to rely on external motivators. We all need money. That money motivates is not in question, but if it comes in the form of minimal increases, toughly negotiated and reluctantly given, it motivates minimally.

CARROT AND STICK

Ever since work began, people have resorted to a combination of threat and reward to get other people to do what they want. If we go far enough back in history to the time of slavery, it was all stick and no carrot. As time went on carrots were introduced in the hope that people would perform better, and they did, by a little for a while. So next we tried washing the carrots, cooking them and providing bigger ones too, and we tried padding the stick or even hiding it, pretending we didn't have one, until we needed it once more. Again performance improved – a little.

At present we are faced with economic constraints on pay increases and there are ever fewer opportunities for promotion. We are desperate for higher performance and we are running out of carrots. The stick is increasingly being seen as politically incorrect. So the motivation system is failing us, but not a moment too soon, and besides it never worked that well anyway. People at work by and large do not perform up to their potential, as a glance at how well they can perform in a real emergency readily shows.

The carrot and stick analogy originates from donkey motivation. In my memory the performance of donkeys is hardly inspiring. I hope I am not doing donkeys an injustice if I say that in fact they will do as little as they can get away with. If we treat people like donkeys, they will perform like donkeys. We must fundamentally change our ideas about motivation. If people are really going to perform, they must be self-motivated.

Research has consistently shown that both job security and the quality of life in the workplace have a higher priority for a considerable proportion of people. When either or both of these internal motivators are absent, money, the most obvious external motivator, takes on a greater significance because 'It's the only thing we can get here, so we'll fight for every penny we can get.' However, if money is perceived, given and received as a measure of self-worth, there is a fairly logical explanation for its higher significance.

MOTIVATION AND MASLOW

In the 1950s an American psychologist, Abraham Maslow, broke the mold of delving into pathology to try to understand human nature. Instead, he studied mature, complete, successful and fulfilled people, and concluded that we could all be that way. In fact, he asserted that this was the natural human state. All we had to do, in his opinion, was to overcome our inner blocks to our development and maturity. Maslow was the father of the more optimistic wave of psychological thinking that is still in the process of displacing behaviorism as the favored model of humans. Psychological optimism is essential if we are fully to embrace coaching as the management style of the future.

Maslow is best known in business circles for his hierarchy of human needs. This model suggests that the most basic need is for food and water, and that we will care for little else (except possibly a mobile phone!) until that

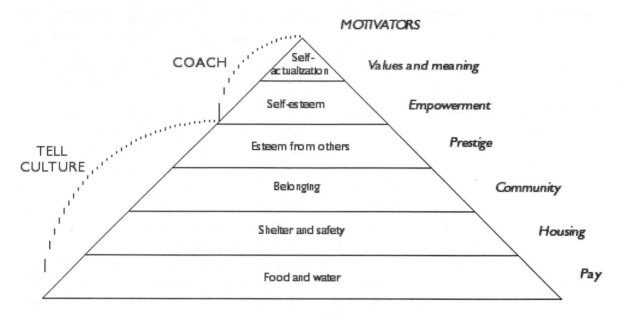

MOTIVATORS

COACH

Self-actualization — Values and meaning

Self-esteem — Empowerment

Esteem from others — Prestige

TELL CULTURE

Belonging — Community

Shelter and safety — Housing

Food and water — Pay

MASLOW'S HIERARCHY OF NEEDS

need is met. Once we have secured a supply of food and water, we begin to concern ourselves with items such as shelter, clothing and safety. Again, when we have these, at least in part, we begin to focus on our social needs, as Maslow described it the need to belong to a grouping. These needs are met in part by our family, but later we also meet them by joining clubs and associations.

Next we seek to satisfy our desire for the esteem of others, by display and by competing with them for power, victory or recognition. This extroverting need is eventually displaced by a subtler esteem need, the need for self-esteem. Here we demand higher standards of ourselves, and look to our own criteria by which we measure ourselves, rather than to how others see us.

Maslow's highest state was the self-actualizing person who emerges when both the esteem needs are satisfied and the individual is no longer driven by the need to prove themselves, either to themselves or to anyone else. He called this self-actualiz*ing* because self-actualiz*ed* would have implied that we could really arrive there, whereas he saw it as a never-ending journey. The need associated with self-actualizers is the need for meaning and purpose in their lives. They want their work, their activities and their existence to have some value, to be a contribution to others.

MOTIVATION AT WORK

How does all this relate to motivation? People will seek to engage in those activities that help them to meet their needs. They are likely to be only partially conscious of this process, because work has naturally developed in ways that do help to meet those needs. However, the more our motivation systems are geared to the *levels* of needs of those we wish to motivate, the happier everyone is going to be.

Work does meet people's primary needs by giving them an income with which they can feed, water and clothe their families and pay their housing costs. Tied housing in the past and the staff canteen also help to take care of those needs. Work brings people together into a work community. Furthermore, work offers promotion, prestige, pay grades and even a company car in which to solicit the esteem of others. The normal motivator used in work, rewards in various currencies, goes some of the way to meeting the survival needs, the belonging needs and even the lower of the two esteem needs. Very clever so far.

A glance into history will reveal that a few decades ago there was a far greater emphasis on tied housing and work social and sports clubs than there is today, and far less on promotion and prestige. In other words, society today is collectively seeking need satisfaction slightly higher up the hierarchy. Reward systems are beginning to reflect the changes at that level.

The next need toward which a large segment of modern society is beginning to move is that for self-esteem. Traditional business and management methods are very poorly equipped to meet that need. In fact, they fail to do so principally because the very nature of self-esteem runs counter to them.

From time to time economic downturns, downsizing, job insecurity, minimal pay increases and declining house prices lead large numbers of workers to go back down the hierarchy. When this occurs, the spectrum of predominant needs becomes broader. Worse still, many businesses can no longer easily supply those things that attract the esteem of others, such as promotion and company cars. So how will businesses motivate their people? They must continue to meet the basic needs while making the fundamental changes necessary to enable them to meet employees' emerging higher needs.

COACHING IS ESSENTIAL

Self-esteem is not met by prestige and privilege, which are more symbolic than substantial. It is built when someone is seen to be worthy of making choices. Promotion without genuine empowerment and the opportunity to express potential is counterproductive. While telling negates choice, disempowers, limits potential and demotivates, coaching does the opposite.

CORPORATE VALUES AND THE FUTURE

Some employees, especially younger ones, are showing signs of possessing the needs of self-actualizers. They want their work to be of value and to have meaning and purpose. Lining the pockets of shareholders is no longer seen as meaningful. Companies are being obliged to consider more carefully their ethics and values and the needs of all their stakeholders, employees, customers, the community and the environment.

This issue is being raised more and more frequently by staff and managers on the courses we run. Companies are seeking a change of management style, but employees are demanding it. If these young and, in Maslow's terms, more mature employees are not to become disaffected, the changes will have to get under way soon. They will inevitably take time, and there is not much time left. So little time, in fact, and so important is this issue that in this edition I have added the next three chapters to address it more fully. It is destined to become a key realm for coaches and it demands a deeper level of understanding.

CHOICE OF MANAGEMENT BEHAVIOR

Self-esteem is the lifeblood of performance at work

Of the four criteria that cause us to choose our management behavior, the development of our staff gets the lowest priority. At the head of the list comes time pressure, then fear, next comes the quality of the job or the product, leaving staff development a poor fourth. Shortage of time and excess fear drive us into command and control, while the quality of work and the need for development demand coaching.

It comes as little surprise that coaching is sidelined by short-termism and the urgency of shareholder return. However, the wake-up call is sounding, and that is the changing expectations of younger staff. At job interviews they want to know what training and development opportunities and what management style they can expect. They do not seek – nor do they want – a job for life, and they will leave if their needs are not met. And those needs are for things that will help their self-belief, such as a coaching management style.

This notion is further supported by a glance at where many bright young staff have reached on Maslow's hierarchy of needs – the self-esteem level. The majority of our postindustrial western society is still in the status and recognition phase, and that includes many executives. There are two problems with this. One is that bosses assume that their staff are either in the same phase or below them in the hierarchy, and therefore do not recognize the importance of self-esteem to their workers. The other is that staff lose respect for bosses who appear to be less psychologically evolved. The need for status and their command-and-control behavior become the butt of jokes or scorn.

Self-belief is a very useful yardstick against which to assess the impact of our behavior on others. It is far easier, if more painful, to look at our interventions with others in terms of how they enhance or damage the other's self-belief. All instruction, all criticism, every reduction in choice, every manifestation of hierarchy, every act of secrecy subtly lowers people's self-belief. Coaching, trust, openness, respect, authentic praise, freedom of choice and, of course, success raise it.

14

Coaching for Purpose

I mentioned at the end of the previous chapter how self-actualizers seek meaning and purpose and very often find it by contributing to others in some way. More and more people are seeming to care as much about fairness and the plight of others as they do about themselves. These emerging altruistic concerns may also cause them to question corporate ethics and values and the profit motive. It is not surprising, therefore, that global investment in what are called 'ethical' funds is increasing fast, and that sexism and racism, previously endemic in many workplaces, are now widely condemned.

The drive for these changes is coming from ordinary people who want more say in how they are treated at work and by business. However, the 'warming' environment is also sending all of us, and business in particular, some harsh messages about our values and behavior in the global context. In addition, the potential consequences of the intensive farming of animals and genetic modification of crops are forcing serious re-evaluation of agricultural methods that is way beyond the province of mere 'nature lovers'. What will the next beachhead be?

I cannot fail to notice on coaching programs that the issue of meaning and purpose is being raised more and more often. I am amazed how frequently participants choose as the subject of practice coaching sessions their desire to escape what they see as the meaningless corporate world and go independent. Countered by their need for security they may well choose to stay put for a time, but while dissatisfaction haunts them how well will they really perform?

Coaching is an invaluable tool in this environment for helping staff clarify their own thoughts, since so long as they remain confused and frustrated they are unlikely to give of their best. Some may leave the organization anyway, but most can learn how to find meaning in their existing work, and thereby achieve better performance with far greater willingness and satisfaction.

I list below the sort of coaching questions I use in these situations, always bearing in mind that in practice, my next question will invariably be determined by the answer I received to the previous one. I am assuming that the coachee in this case has already indicated that he wishes to work on improving the quality of his work life.

GOAL

I always try to start positively and with the coachee's goal – the ideal for him.

❏ What would you like to have by the end of this coaching session?
❏ Let's imagine a year or so into the future. What would your ideal work situation be? Describe to me in some detail what your typical working day would be like. (This may be in or out of his current job, with no judgment on my part.)
❏ What are the elements of that scenario that you yearn for most at this time?
❏ How important is each of these to you? (You could use a 1–10 scale.)
❏ So your goal at work would be what?
❏ By when would you want that to be the case?

❏ Deep down, what do you really want from your work life?

❏ If that seems a bit of a stretch from where you are now, give me a couple of stepping stones along the way.

❏ From where you are now, what would be a first step that you could feel good about?

REALITY

❏ How much of this situation do you feel is within your control? (Frequently it is a big issue for coachees to realize that ultimately their situation is their choice. They so often feel a victim and therefore experience themselves as powerless.)

❏ Aside from the day-to-day frustrations, what is it about your work that gives you the most dissatisfaction?

❏ What is the concern that lies behind the dissatisfaction?

❏ What sort of thing could meet that concern?

❏ What else bothers you? And what else? Tell me more about that.

❏ What sort of people and what sort of activities at work do you dislike?

❏ For how much of your time at work do you feel positive and how much negative? Let's look at the positive.

❏ What sort of people and activites do you enjoy most at work?

❏ What is it about those people and those activities that you like?

❏ What qualities do they represent? Where else do you find those qualities?

❏ What activities in or out of work are meaningful to you?

❏ If you had to state a purpose for your life, what would it be?

❏ If you had the opportunity to write your obituary now, what would you like to be writing about your life? (A good one, but be careful who you use it with!)

OPTIONS

❏ What options do you have for changing things? (If the coachee answers 'I could change my job', continue as follows but bear in mind that changing forms and structures does not change anything. It is consciousness that must change.)

❏ What would be the benefits of doing that? What would you lose?

❏ How might you ensure that the same problems would not arise in a new job?

❏ What sort of job? How would you find it? How secure would that be?

❏ So changing jobs and going independent are two options. Let's now look at how you might introduce some of those qualities you seek into your current work.

❏ How else? Where? And where else?

❏ What would have to change? What could you do to change that? Who could you ask to have other parts changed?

❏ If you were able to change all those things, how well would your needs be met?

This is by no means an exhaustive set of questions, but I hope it does provide a line of questioning that you might usefully pursue in sessions of this nature. The above are intentionally not all phrased as questions in order to illustrate a way of avoiding the inquisitorial effect of every sentence ending with a question mark.

Eventually we would get to a set of WILL questions to tie the coachee down to real action, either within the current job or elsewhere, but without the coach's influence or prejudice either way. We always have to remember that the coachee's self-belief is paramount, so succeeding and making his own choices about how to do so are also paramount.

15
Coaching for Meaning

Man's search for meaning is the primary motivation in his life and not a secondary rationalisation of instinctual drives.
(Viktor Frankl, Man's Search for Meaning, 1959)

Maslow contributed more than just his hierarchy – he was one of the founders of humanistic psychology, sometimes known as the third force of psychology that emerged after psychoanalysis and behaviorism. Instead of studying mental illness and pathology as others had done before, he studied healthy, fully functioning people to gain a deeper insight into human nature.

The goal of humanistic psychology was the fulfillment of human potential through self-awareness, seen by some as a panacea for all ills, and it valued the emotions. It penetrated the business world in a limited way in the 1970s and influenced the trend toward personal development, although it was not until 1995 that Daniel Goleman's book on the subject made emotional intelligence not only acceptable but desirable to the point of necessity for success in business. Everyone began to want some.

Emotional intelligence can be described as interpersonal intelligence or, even more simply, as social skills. This can be divided into five domains: knowing one's emotions (self-awareness), managing one's emotions, motivating oneself,

EMOTIONAL INTELLIGENCE

recognizing emotions in others and handling relationships. That sounds straightforward enough and we all combine these skills to some degree. Emotionally intelligent people just embody them more fully than others.

No sooner had we swallowed EQ, as it became known, than several new books appeared advocating the merits of SQ or spiritual intelligence. Spiritual in this sense is not a religious concept but is defined by author Elisabeth Denton as 'the basic desire to find ultimate meaning and purpose in one's life and to live an integrated life'.

All of these give credence to the notion that many people in business today are facing a real crisis of meaning. In her book *Spiritual Intelligence*, Danah Zohar quotes a 36-year-old businessman describing his personal crisis:

I am managing a large and successful company here in Sweden. I have good health; I have a wonderful family, a position in the community. I suppose I have 'power'. But still I am not certain what I am doing with my life. I am not certain I am on the right path doing the job that I do.

He explained that he was very worried about the state of the world, especially the condition of the global environment and the breakdown of the community. He felt people were avoiding the real scale of the problems facing them. Big businesses like his were especially guilty of not addressing such problems. 'I want to do something about it,' he continued. 'I want, if you like, to use my life to serve, but I don't know how. I just know that I want to be part of the solution. Not the problem.'

THE DEVELOPMENT OF MEANING AND PURPOSE

The idea that meaning and purpose are significant is far from new, in fact it is probably as old as the most ancient religion. Perhaps the time is now right for it to be fully recognized in the business world – but it needs to arise from within, since imposing it from outside is seldom effective, as coaches well know.

Business and life coaches are going to need additional skills and training to be able to address such deeper issues effectively and comfortably. Many years ago my wife and I were both drawn to the depth and inclusiveness of psychosynthesis, which has informed my coaching work ever since. She now runs a psychosynthesis educational charity.

Psychosynthesis was conceived by Dr Roberto Assagioli in 1911. He had been a student of Freud and was the first Freudian psychoanalyst in Italy. Like Carl Jung, his friend and fellow student, he rebelled against Freud's limited pathological and animalistic vision of man. Both suggested that we possess a higher nature and Assagioli asserted that much of the psychological dysfunction in the world stems from frustration or even desperation about the lack of meaning and purpose in our lives.

Assagioli was far ahead of his time and psychosynthesis remained relatively obscure until the 1960s, when it became a primary component of the emerging fourth force of psychology known as transpersonal psychology. It does not negate the third force (humanistic psychology) but embraces and builds on it. It adds a deeper sense of the will, the experience of meaning, purpose and direction, personal responsibility and placing others before self – all based on the hypothesis that we each have a deeper identity or a higher organizing principle.

Psychosynthesis offers a number of maps and models, the strands of which weave a very useful cradle for in-depth coaching. It provides a simple model of human development that, like all models, is not the truth but merely a representation that enables a conversation to occur within our own minds and with others. If it is even partially correct, it suggests that coaches may have a great deal of work on their hands in the coming years.

A psychosynthesis-trained coach may invite the coachee to reframe life as a developmental journey, to see the creative potential within each problem, to see obstacles as stepping stones and to imagine that we all have a purpose in life with challenges and obstacles to overcome in order to fulfill that purpose. The coach's questions will seek the coachee's recognition of the positive potential in the issue and the actions he chooses to take.

THE SPIRITUAL JOURNEY

We can trace our experience of our own life track or that of others on a two-dimensional graphical model, of which the horizontal axis represents material success and psychological integration and the vertical axis represents spiritual, value or aspirational unfolding.

Let's consider an example of each from a psychosynthesis text:

A business person may be focused on personal achievement and success in the material world and may have become a well-integrated person, a good parent and a respected member of society, without ever having asked themselves a meaningful question about life. This is the tendency of western people, which has resulted in great material progress and innovation.

They may be scornful of the more mystical type who leads a contemplative and ascetic life but who seems ill-equipped to cope with the realities and essentials of the everyday world. These people live a monastic life of study and of gentle assistance to others. Their home, their finances and even their personality may be in a bit of a mess. However, they see the business person's pursuits as being pointless, ego driven and often destructive to themselves and to others. This is the eastern path; although given the economic growth of the East of late, these geographical distinctions are liable to be confusing.

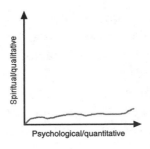

There can be little argument that western people have focused their energies on moving along the horizontal axis and have done so with gusto and to good effect.

Western influence and economic imperatives are now a pervasive global force but, in pockets in both East and West, there are those who focus on journeying up the vertical axis.

The further we progress along either path to the exclusion of the other, the more we depart from the ideal or balanced path between the two and the tension increases.

If social pressures, business imperatives or blind determination override this tension that is attempting to pull us back on track, we are liable to be stopped by hitting a wake-up wall. This wall is known as the crisis of meaning.

When we hit the crisis wall, we tend to bounce back in shock and into temporary confusion and performance regression for a while, but we are at the same time pulled upwards toward the ideal eventually to discover a more balanced path.

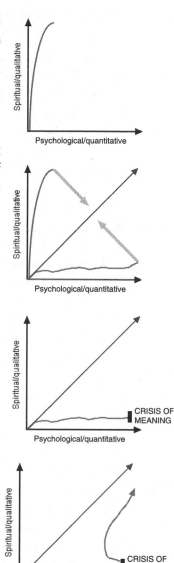

The horizontal axis can also be equated to knowledge. The crisis of meaning occurs when our accumulation of knowledge far exceeds the tempering effect of our values. In the crisis we experience a breakdown of the false sense of security provided by the illusion of power and certainty that great knowledge gives us.

KNOWLEDGE

Wisdom lies beyond knowledge and is deeper. It provides foresight, it is often paradoxical and it offers a different order of security that a person emerging from the crisis is then able to experience. The 45° line in the diagrams above could thus be said to represent wisdom, lying between the extremes of what we might cynically describe as indiscriminately exploited knowledge on one side and ungrounded spiritual fanaticism on the other.

Knowledge is often said to be the valued currency of today and the future. For centuries humanity presided over a land-based economy, then with the Industrial Revolution came a shift to a capital-based one. Land-owning aristocrats gave way to *nouveau riche* merchants. In the new knowledge-based economy the technophiiles may appear to hold sway, but their grip has been proved to be tenuous and they have a long way to fall. Is this an indication that the gap between our knowledge and our wisdom is too great to be sustainable? Could we already be glimpsing the emergence of the next phase, the wisdom-based economy? Can we hope that the politicians and business leaders of the future will be truly wise, or should we rather be looking for wisdom within ourselves, finding our own inner leadership?

FROM PUSH TO PULL

I have omitted one element from the psychosynthesis diagrams above, a point of light that lies beyond the 45° arrowhead. It represents our higher self or soul. It exerts a gentle pull on us to 'get back on track', one that is easily overridden by our more earthbound desires and ambitions. In the past such a notion could easily be dismissed by rational scientific minds as fanciful speculation. However, recent advances in neurobiology have revealed what is called the 'god spot' in the temporal lobes of the brain which, to quote Danah Zohar, could be 'a crucial component of our larger spiritual intelligence'.

Business rightly recognizes that many systems in the world are shifting from push to pull, from prescription to choice. Pulling what we want off the internet superseding blind acceptance of what 'they' want to push on to us is one example, coaching replacing telling as a management style is another.

In-depth coaching is an invaluable resource for helping people to clear away their defensive shields and self-imposed blockages, so that they can more readily experience their own inner guidance. Hearing and obeying the 'still small voice within' early enough may be a good way to avert a crisis and coaching can certainly contribute to that.

COACHING THROUGH THE CRISIS OF MEANING

I cannot attempt to go into detail here about the techniques and potential pitfalls of coaching people through a major crisis of meaning. It can be a profound experience and an unsettling time for people who have traveled a long way along the horizontal plane before it occurs. I strongly advocate some training in psychosynthesis or a similar psychology for independent coaches who wish to enter this field. It is an area that is likely to be beyond the brief time avaiilability, experience or capability of what we might describe as a normal coach/manager.

Of course, a crisis is not a prerequisite for psycho-spiritual development. Some people travel far along their journey with neither a crisis nor a coach. Other progress with less dramatic consequences through a series of mini-crises and the bends are not as acute. To coach such a person, normal high-quality coaching training should be adequate. In fact under almost all circumstances, if a coach sticks tightly to non-prescriptive principles and follows the coachee's agenda, little can go wrong. A problem only arises when a coach, unaccustomed to extreme outbursts and sudden swings of emotion, panics and intervenes to try to help the person to control their feelings. The coachee needs to enter into and, if necessary, relive residual suppressed emotions at his own pace, albeit with process guidance and protection.

Coaching someone through a crisis of meaning is seldom a one-stop journey; a series of sessions over a period of several months is likely to be required. In addition, after his company has invested money and time in his in-depth coaching, the individual may in the end decide to leave his job and find alternative work more in tune with his newly identified and clarified purpose.

It might be simpler for some businesses to keep their head in the corporate sand as a way out of the complexities of meaning and purpose. In the long run, however, I believe that those businesses that stand by their people in their hour of need will have that goodwill returned many times over.

16

Coaching the Corporation

While this book is about coaching, it would be an omission not to acknowledge the broader business and social conditions that make coaching such a valuable skill. How will we manage in the future? Will we revert to command and control when the pendulum swings back? Is there a pendulum at all? Where is business going? Perhaps it is inexorably traveling an evolutionary journey of which the direction, if not the timing, is reasonably predictable.

George Orwell, Stanley Kubrick and even Alvin Toffler would tell us that prediction is a risky business, but when the signs are strong enough it does no harm to be aware of the possibilities. Since changing the management culture of a large multinational business takes many years, it is vital for its leaders to look into the future.

One way of doing this is to explore whether an individual's process of psychological development can tell us anything about the direction in which companies are going. Indeed, the central platform of Arie de Geus's groundbreaking book *The Living Company* is that companies are and act like living beings.

Can businesses experience the same kind of crisis of meaning that many individuals are currently undergoing? I suggest that they can and they do. And could it be more widespread still? Could the global business community be approaching a collective crisis of meaning? Some telltale signs are here. Economic indicators are no longer providing clear signals of what is happening. Both corporate ethics and the environment are posing unprecedented challenges to business. Anti-globalization and anti-capitalism protestors have greeted every gathering of global leaders recently. The rich are still getting richer while the poor are getting poorer.

The UK has led the way in attempting to address the last problem by writing off some third world debt, an idea that was unthinkable when Fidel Castro suggested it a decade ago. Bill Gates, the ultimate marketeer, has now recognized that computers do not keep people alive and is setting an example by generously funding a global immunization program.

GLOBALIZATION

A special edition of Newsweek devoted to issues that would dominate the world in 2001 identified globalization as the main influence. There were two related concerns: that private business will have to carry more of the public burden in trying to repair social problems, and that the market is not the answer to everything. Claude Smadja of the World Economic Forum wrote:

Private companies must assert a much wider and stronger sense of corporate social responsibility. And we must listen to the responsible voices of a new 'civil society' ... The rise of NGOs also reflects increased public disenchantment with all *institutions – governments, corporations, international organizations, media.*

Michael Hirsh of Newsweek commented that the debate is less about privatizing the public sector than the converse, 'publicizing' the private sector. Manny Armadi, CEO of Cause & Effect Marketing in the UK, expressed it this way:

The burden of economic fundamentals is now such that government on its own can't fulfill its social obligations. On the other side, the sheer power and influence of businesses in the economy is now huge.

When asked if he thought people were entitled to hold the leaders of such enterprises accountable for their behavior, he replied, 'Absolutely.'

Globalization and instant, frequent communication around the world are blurring the space and time distinctions between 'us' and 'them'. At the same time, our continually, though some would argue slowly, maturing consciousness is causing us to extend our area of concern to include within 'us' people, countries and cultures that a decade ago we would certainly have regarded as 'them'. Thus both external forces and our inner development are conspiring to break down barriers and persuade us to accept and embrace the common destiny that all people share – and share responsibility for.

So if the public is calling for more corporate social responsibility and inspiring business leaders are talking about it, why is so little of it happening? What is the sticking point? Deborah Holmes of Ernst & Young confirmed something I have observed on many of my coaching courses when she said:

You can have very enlightened practices in the heads of the top leaders, and employees hungry for enlightened practices. And then managers are operating the way they always have, not understanding that there's anything more to their responsibility than a good profit-and-loss statement.

Clearly, these issues were around well before the devastating attack on the World Trade Center in New York on 11 September 2001. However, for many individuals, businesses and nations, that event triggered new and even deeper consideration of personal and collective

CORPORATE SOCIAL RESPONSIBILITY

responsibility and may have accelerated the changes already envisaged by earlier commentators.

The summarizing heading of a *Financial Times* article on 20 September (written before the attack) is 'A reconnection with core values: Greed is not good in the new age of business: Workers are more than the sum of their parts: Spirituality in business: Stephen Overell joins the search for the ultimate competitive advantage, and finds that companies are trying to offer staff meaning and purpose'.

Jim McNish, head of executive development at retail group Kingfisher, is quoted in the article as saying, 'Human beings want to love their organisations – they don't want to work for a set of bastards. People seek meaning in their work and will start to creep out the door if they find none.' Ken Costa, vice-chairman of banking group UBS Warburg, makes a similar point: 'You can see the frustration. It demonstrates itself in uncertainty and a lack of fulfilment and ultimately leads people to leave an organisation. More are leaving to work in the voluntary sector … In the last round of graduate recruitment we did, a surprising amount of people asked "what are your policies regarding social responsibility". That has never happened before.'

Many people believe that a major shift in the attitude and role of business is inevitable and in fact is already under way, driven in large measure by public demand. People are signifying that they will no longer tolerate being in service to the economy; instead they are demanding that the economy be made to serve people. Will this come about by a series of managed course corrections as businesses learn to accept their responsibility, their true meaning and purpose, or will they continue their blinkered pursuit of wealth at any price until they run into barricades manned by ordinary people with higher demands and aspirations?

Changes in ethics and values in society and in business affect a wide range of aspects of business relating to both people and products:

❑ The way staff are treated and management style.
❑ Treatment of the environment, such as waste and recycling.

❏ The way suppliers are treated, particularly those in developing countries.

❏ Fair remuneration for all, with an eye to executive excesses.

❏ Concerns about aggressive selling and misleading advertising.

❏ Internal and external openness and honesty.

❏ Health and welfare considerations for staff, including stress, the demands of parenting and so on.

❏ Sexual equality, positive racial attitudes and avoidance of harrassment.

❏ Executives expected to be role models and set examples.

❏ Products that offer genuine value.

❏ Products that are socially beneficial, or at least neutral.

❏ Products that put people before profit.

❏ Concerns over the use of hazardous or environmentally dangerous chemicals.

❏ How the company relates to the wider community.

A company that disregards any of these areas is at risk of criticism and needs to bear in mind that even what is acceptable today may not be so tomorrow. A company with vision, however, will not just be keeping pace with the public mood but will want to be ahead of it, particularly because it realizes that it has a responsibility to society.

COACHING FOR CULTURE CHANGE

A listening, learning, coaching culture may provide the best chance of riding out the unsettling waves of change that businesses are facing. Businesses can adopt a more supportive, people-oriented culture, one in which coaching is commonplace, downwards, with peers and even upwards. In this way staff's needs are acknowledged and they are helped by coaching to clarify their direction for themselves, while at the same time the coach/manager learns a great deal about their wishes and hopes. If managers listen to their people and act on what they hear, employees will be happier and perform better and staff turnover will plummet. On the other hand if they only pay lip service to this, they will have raised expectations only to dash them again and will have made things worse than they were before.

In addition to this management style change, companies are likely to be called on to live up to the values and ethics they so boldly claim in their mission statements. If they don't, they may be taken to task by their staff and their customers. Both are liable to vote with their feet. Companies providing products and services that make a genuine contribution to society offer meaningful employment by their very nature. Those whose products and services are questionable or downright harmful are most likely to fall foul of staff seeking meaning and purpose at work.

On this scale few companies are wholly black and few wholly white. The majority are a shade of gray. The wiser ones can and do compensate for any perceived failings in various ways, for example by contributing to the local community or lending staff to social projects.

Why is coaching so important in this? Because a value-based future cannot be prescribed by some outside authority. Performance will always be at its best when staff, shareholders, directors and even customers share the same values, but before that can happen staff need to be encouraged to find out what their own values are.

Once we accept that we need to change the culture of our business to incorporate a coaching ethos, where do we start? With the people or with the company? The answer must be both. Imposing democracy and demanding cooperation are unacceptable contradictions.

Here are a few guidelines:

❏ If we redesign our company structure too radically or too quickly, we are liable to get too far ahead of our staff.
❏ If we impose a redesign on our staff, they are liable to object even if it is intended to be entirely for their benefit.
❏ We must first help staff develop themselves and through coaching experiment with some of the attitudes and behaviors that we expect in the new organization.
❏ Executives and senior management must, from the very

beginning, set an example and model the ideal attitudes and behaviors authentically and well.

❏ Staff cannot be forced to change, but need the opportunity to choose how to change.

❏ Without a collective vision change cannot succeed, but without vision at the top it will not even start.

When coaching the board members of a company going through culture change, we must first help them to become clear about what they require from the change and what it involves, and ensure that they are fully committed to seeing it through. This is likely to require an investment of time that board members are often reluctant to make because of short-term pressures. However, lasting and effective change is only a pipe dream without the commitment of the board, or at the very least of one key member of it who acts as a champion. The willingness to see change through is vital to avoid staff becoming disillusioned if grand plans come to nothing.

The approach we take at Performance Consultants is then to institute a very thorough program of maintenance and reinforcement from day one to support managers' initial exposure to coaching and the accompanying management style changes expected of them. Every member of staff in any supervisory role must go through a basic coaching skills course to ensure that a new common language is quickly established. The rest of the staff will also need at least an explanation and some exposure to the principles of coaching so that they are not confused or suspicious of any behavioral changes on the part of managers.

Other components of culture change maintenance include regular updates, supervision, buddy sharing, feedback, assessment, appraisals and support of many kinds. The more these are internally designed and staffed the better. We prefer to train 'master coaches' within the organization to do this rather than undertaking it ourselves because then ownership lies where it needs to be – within the company.

THE COACHING APPROACH

17
Feedback and Assessment

The worst feedback is personal and judgmental.
The most effective is subjective and descriptive.

So far we have considered coaching as a tool for addressing existing issues of planning, problem solving, reviewing, skill development and the like, and we have considered the broader context of meaning and purpose at work. In this chapter I am going to demonstrate a way of using coaching for giving feedback, and for self and team assessment and development.

FEEDBACK

We can identify five levels of feedback that are in common use. They are illustrated below in order from A, the least helpful, to E, the most productive and the only one of the five that promotes major learning and performance benefits. The other four at best produce minimal short-term improvement, and at worst cause further decline in performance and self-esteem. The first four are widely used in business circles and at first glance seem reasonable – that is, until or unless they are examined with care.

A. Manager's exclamation: *'You are useless.'*
This is a **personalized criticism** that devastates self-esteem and confidence and is bound to make future performance even worse. It contains nothing helpful.

B. Manager's intervention: *'This report is useless.'*
This **judgmental comment** directed at the report, not at the person, also damages the performer's self-esteem, though less badly, but it still provides no information on which the writer can act to correct it.

C. Manager's intervention: *'The content of your report was clear and concise, but the layout and presentation were too down-market for its target readership.'*
This avoids criticism and provides the performer with **some information** on which to act, but in insufficient detail and it **generates no ownership**.

D. Manager's intervention: *'How do you feel about the report?'*
The performer now has ownership, but is likely to give a non-response such as 'Fine', or to make a **value judgment** of the work such as 'Great' or 'Lousy', rather than a more useful description.

E. Manager's interventions: *'What is the essential purpose of your report?' 'To what extent do you think this draft achieves that?' 'What are the other points you feel need to be emphasized?' 'Who do you see as the target reader?'* etc.
In response to a series of questions such as these, **the performer/learner gives a detailed, non-judgmental description** of the report and the thinking behind it.

So why does the form of feedback illustrated in E dramatically accelerate learning and improve performance? Only E meets all the best coaching criteria. In order to answer the manager's questions in E, the performer/learner is compelled to engage his brain and get involved. He has to recollect and formulate his thoughts before he can articulate his responses. This is AWARENESS. It helps him to learn how to evaluate his own work and thereby become more self-reliant. This way he 'owns' his performance and his assessment of it. This is RESPONSIBILITY. When these two factors are optimized, learning occurs. Conversely, if the manager just tells the performer his own opinion, the actual engagement of the performer's brain is likely to be minimal, there is no ownership and no means for the manager to measure what has been assimilated.

The use of descriptive rather than judgmental terminology, either by the performer, as seen in E, or by the manager, as in C, avoids evoking the performer's defensiveness. Defensiveness must be avoided because, when it is present, the truth/reality becomes smothered in inaccurate excuses and justifications, which may even be believed by both the performer and the manager and which are no basis for performance improvement. However, in intervention C, as well as in A and B, the manager retains ownership of both the evaluation and the correction, so learning for the future is correspondingly minimized. It can be seen that interventions A–D all fall short of the ideal; nevertheless they are the ones most frequently used in business.

PROCESS AND RESULT

The golf ball provides perfect feedback. It ends up exactly where the golfer puts it

Feedback from ourselves and from others is vital for learning and performance improvement. That feedback needs to cover both the results of the action and the action process itself. For example, where the golf ball lands is the result and the golf swing is the process. The result is easy to determine in sport, but perhaps less easy to measure in business at times. Even in sport, we all too often judge the result of an action, evoking defensive blindness. What we need is the very opposite, an accurate, detailed description of the result. 'The ball was out' is more helpful than 'You blew that one'; better still is 'It was six inches beyond the base line.' We can learn as much from those actions that produce the wrong result as we can from those that give the right one. This feedback can be provided by the coach or the coachee, the latter being by far the best, for reasons covered earlier.

Let's now look at process feedback. A tennis coach may observe a student's forehand swing and comment critically, or preferably descriptively, on what he observes. The feedback he offers is based on the disparity between what he observes and an ideal usually based on his knowledge of the correct way, or on his own way. The observable forehand swing is only the symptom or outward manifestation of a complex array of converging physical and psychological factors that comprise the cause. Any changes to that forehand demanded by the coach will be applied initially at the symptomatic level. Real, lasting change must reach the causal level, better still must be initiated there. The coach is unable to observe the causal level, which resides inside the student. His own high-quality internal feedback is what is ideally required. The student can be made to access this level by raising his physiological and psychological self-awareness. The questions that cause him to do this will only be effective if they follow the feedback principles, which are identical to those used for causing someone to watch the ball.

Feedback relates to the past, the immediate past, for example when coaching in real time for sport, or the longer-term past, which will generally be the case in business. It is, however, the anticipation of the question that causes you to be aware in the present, and it is that immediate awareness that produces physiological efficiency. For example, I can say to a student, 'On the next ball I am going to ask you which part of the movement feels the least comfortable to you.' He will be paying attention to his body while he is making the movement, and as a result the inefficiency may well not occur on the very first occasion. I am equating comfort here with biomechanical efficiency, and more obvious perhaps is the fact that any biomechanical inefficiency will be experienced as discomfort in that area.

This is taking us very close to feedforward, or planning in more common parlance. The feedback principles on the previous pages remain true. Those principles are maintained if you are coaching me and I am compelled to

FEEDFORWARD

describe to you, and therefore to myself, in detail what I am going to do. They are not if you tell me what to do, or even if you ask me whether I know what I am going to do. It will be the quality of effective questions that will determine the quality of the feedforward or planning.

'Who will take this one on?' 'How confident are you that you can complete this on time?' 'Which element of this are you unsure of?' 'What might the obstacles be to achieving this?' 'When can you have it done by?' All these questions generate responsibility and ownership, but they also raise awareness of other factors.

HARD TO CHANGE

Why do we persist in employing the least effective means of feedback? Because we look at it all from our point of view, rather than that of the performer; because we say what we want, without understanding the effects of what we say. Whether that stems from habit, poor role models, hierarchical arrogance or just unthinkingly failing to look beneath the surface will vary from manager to manager. The important thing, if we truly wish to bring the best out of people – ourselves, our staff or even our children – is to rethink and refocus at a fundamental level. Our primary objective must be to understand what the performer/learner needs in order to perform the task well, and to ask, say or do whatever it takes to help them meet that need. Our own wish to be in control or to display our superior knowledge, or simply our laziness to give up old habits and change, will need to be set aside if we want them to perform. It is hard to break the prevailing mold of behavior, but break it we must.

Let's return to our simplest example, watching the tennis ball. It is very important for a tennis player to watch the ball. There is nothing wrong with that. However, telling him to do it does not cause him to do it. On the other hand, and here is the paradox, the number of times the ball revolves is totally unimportant, but if you ask him to try to count them he will be watching the ball. Counting the revolutions is only one of many alternative questions, the choice of which depends on the effect being sought.

Consider another example. A tennis player is alternating between hitting the ball long and into the net. The player can only see her efforts in terms of good and bad, success and failure. She judges herself harshly. Self-esteem, confidence and performance all suffer, as does the quality of her feedback, perhaps made even worse by her turning away in frustration as soon as she knows she has muffed it again. She tries too hard to correct herself, resulting in struggle, stress and a tendency to overcompensate, leading to further failure.

Most tennis coaches will attempt to deal with this by a technical 'correction' – and they are missing the point. They tackle the symptom, not the cause. By far the most frequent cause of erratic shots is poor feedback, either about where the ball is coming from or where it is going to. Assuming the latter in this case, the question a wiser coach might ask is, 'How high over the net did that ball go?' The coach could have the player call out how high over the top of the net in centimeters the ball goes each time. Getting accurate feedback from the result of her action causes automatic self-correction without effort or strife. Letting go of trying to force the correction (the focus is now on the accuracy of the observation) allows the correction to take place effortlessly and subconsciously. The player's total ownership of the correction is maintained. Of course, the exact height in centimeters by which the ball passes over the net is irrelevant, but the player's focus on and mental recording of the results of her actions are highly relevant.

Generating high-quality relevant feedback, as far as possible from within rather than from experts, is essential for continuous improvement, at work, in sport and in all aspects of life.

PRAISE

Praise is another form of feedback. It tends to be sparingly offered and hungrily received in the workplace, where criticism abounds. In this context, any increase in positive and reduction in negative feedback would seem desirable.

When there is not enough of something it seems churlish to cast doubt on its value, but a caution is in order. Praise insincerely or gratuitously given is hollow indeed and does more harm than good, for phoneyness and manipulation are far more readily recognized than the perpetrators realize. They cheapen the perpetrator and damage relationships and trust. Even authentic praise can cause difficulty. The person being praised may surrender their ability and willingness to self-assess to the giver of praise, and thereby increase their dependence on the opinions of others. We need to do the opposite, to build the autonomy and self-reliance of our staff.

Praise must simultaneously be generous, genuine and judicious.

STRENGTHS AND WEAKNESSES

In business speak we hear a lot about identifying strengths and weaknesses of personnel, of processes and of products. We can list the strengths and weaknesses of each of these and indeed of ourselves. We can list other things too, such as the qualities required of a prospective employee, the qualities we would like to foster in a work team or the qualities we would like to develop in ourselves. We can list the functions of our organization, a department or an individual. We can list technical skills, interpersonal skills or manual skills required. Breaking things down into more detail like this is one level of awareness raising.

We can use this list to take awareness raising a step further if we then rate these strengths, weaknesses, qualities, functions or skills on our now familiar 1–10 scale, either in terms of what we would like them to be, or in terms of what we think they are now.

APPRAISALS

Appraisal systems are common, unpopular, misused, limiting and yet necessary. In a learning, no-blame culture, they can be very beneficial to all concerned. When they categorize only past performance and not future potential, or are judgmental and not descriptive, they are beneficial to no one. Circumstances and company objectives and history are so varied that I would not attempt to suggest any universal appraisal system. However, such a system cannot be far wrong if it is in tune with the above principles of feedback, and the principles of self-assessment that follow.

SELF-ASSESSMENT

Much importance is attached in business to assessing others – peers, subordinates or even bosses – but self-assessment is, in my opinion, the most productive form of assessment. Ratings on skills and qualities given by and to others are best regarded as feedback, valuable stuff on which we can choose to act, rather than as a judgment or the truth, which may have a disempowering impact on us. A video, on the other hand, does show the reality of what happened on that one occasion, but should be used for information to a person rather than criticism of them. Self-assessment bypasses the negative effects of criticism and maintains responsibility where it needs to be for effective action and self-improvement. Let me give an example.

I could list the qualities and skills I would most need to do my job well in random order of importance as the following. In the first column opposite each I could write how I rate myself, and in the second column I could write the rating I could reasonably hope to develop myself to.

QUALITIES

	As I am now	Target
Communicative	8	9
Empathetic	6	9
Patient	7	9
Computer literate	4	7
Administratively capable	6	8
Enthusiastic	8	8
Alert and observant	8	9
Book-keeping competency	5	7

In doing this I have certainly raised my self-awareness, but in terms of the coaching process I have done more than that.

The first column represents the REALITY and the second a realistic, specific, measurable, positively stated, challenging GOAL. All I need to do is to select which one I want to work on, put in a time frame and I will have completed the first two stages of a simple self-coaching process.

I need to take some time to list all the OPTIONS I have for developing my chosen skill or quality. If I have selected a quality, I might want to list the positive behaviors associated with people who have an abundance of that quality. The reason for this is that action steps will usually take the form of new behaviors, rather than new qualities that take longer to develop. In time it is the success of these new behaviors that will enable me to rate myself more highly in terms of the underlying quality.

Finally I will ask myself the WILL questions and present myself with an action plan.

TEAM ASSESSMENT

Variations of this exercise can be used on oneself, on individuals and with teams. It is particularly interesting to have team members list desirable team qualities and then rate their team on each. The disparity between the figures offers opportunities to discuss the different criteria by which people judge and the different experiences that different members have of the same team.

For example, a team of five were asked to list the four most important team qualities in their eyes. Their lists turned out as follows:

JOE	MIKE	SUSAN	VALERIE	DAVID
Humor	Trust	Support	Cooperation	Tolerance
Patience	Courage	Flexibility	Trust	Cohesion
Support	Cooperation	Enthusiasm	Compatibility	Trust
Friendship	Adaptability	Unselfishness	Support	Commitment

From these lists a merged list was formed. Cooperation and cohesion were considered to be the same, as were adaptability and flexibility. Each of the team members was asked to rate the team on each quality. They were asked to do this individually on paper before the figures were brought to the flip chart, so that no member's figures were influenced by the figures of others. The result was as follows:

	JOE	MIKE	SUSAN	VALERIE	DAVID	**Average**
Support	7	8	4	6	6	6.2
Cooperation	8	7	8	6	9	7.6
Trust	7	5	5	7	5	5.8
Adaptability	9	7	8	9	6	7.8
Patience	7	8	4	6	8	6.6
Friendship	9	9	7	5	4	6.8
Commitment	8	8	9	8	8	8.2
Courage	5	6	7	7	8	6.6
Humor	8	6	3	4	5	5.2
Enthusiasm	7	7	8	6	7	7.0
Compatibility	6	6	6	7	6	6.2
Unselfishness	8	7	6	8	6	7.0
Tolerance	7	6	6	6	5	6.0

In this case they were not asked to add to the above ratings a highly personal figure, their rating of how much of each of these qualities they personally contribute to the party. Nor were they asked to rate each other's contribution to the sum total of these qualities in the team. Ratings of this kind can open up huge discussions, disputes, love affairs and several cans of worms, but if I were to work with a team that was going for gold or on whom my life depended, I would want to do this and more!

What the above figures do show is that trust is an issue that needs to be worked on, that Joe's brand of humor is not much appreciated, particularly by the women, that at times Susan feels got at and that David feels isolated. There is plenty of scope for individual coaching here, by a peer or by an outside facilitator, and for a team discussion of OPTIONS and a team agreement of what action steps they WILL take to raise the level of several of these qualities.

Coaching to build qualities in teams or individuals is a way of positively framing weaknesses and is far more creative

**REFRAMING
WEAKNESSES**

Coaching offers personal control. A primary cause of stress in the workplace is a lack of personal control

and likely to achieve success than attempting to exorcise the weakness. This is further reinforcement of the desirability of putting GOAL setting ahead of REALITY in the coaching sequence. There are an infinite number of variations of coaching exercises that can be devised out of this basic model, and examples to suit all kinds of situations. Over to you.

18

The Development of a Team

A small number of people with complementary skills committed to a common purpose, performance goals and ways of working together for which they hold themselves mutually accountable.
(Katzenbach & Smith, The Wisdom of Teams)

We have begun to explore ways of coaching with a team to improve its performance, but we need to understand some of the dynamics of team development if we are to get the best out of its members. I use a simple three-stage model that is easy to understand and where each stage is readily recognized in most teams. More complex and sophisticated models exist, but they are of less practical use, in my experience.

For the purposes of this model the number of team members can range from a handful to a nationful. Teams of more than 15 or 20 members are likely to be made up of subteams, but whether it is a first team or a sub-sub-subteam, certain characteristics remain the same.

HIGH-PERFORMING TEAMS

The model I use blends well with the team-qualities exercise in the previous chapter. Using the views of those team members, for example, we could safely say that an effective, high-performing team would be well endowed with:

Support	Cooperation
Trust	Adaptability
Patience	Friendship
Commitment	Courage
Humor	Enthusiasm
Compatibility	Unselfishness

A team that could reasonably be rated at ten on each of these qualities would indeed be a high-performing team, and an exceptional one. So how can one get a team into such a state? Some people would say with the right chemistry and a lot of luck. Others might not be so convinced that it would be such a great team, because they believe that some internal friction and competition generate good performance. They believe that, but only because they have never seen anything better. Rare as they may be, both in business and in sport, such teams do exist, however.

LUCK OR JUDGMENT

While high-performing teams have, in the past, often come about by luck, some have been developed by dint of the understanding and efforts of the team members and their leader. One such team was the Great Britain field-hockey team which won the gold medal at the Seoul Olympics in 1988. The coach who was largely responsible for their team development was David Whitaker, with whom I now work closely in business. He said of the team: 'They became a harmonious, dynamic unit without negating the special individual talents that each player contributed.'

STAGES OF TEAM DEVELOPMENT

The first demand on a team leader is to understand fully the stages through which a team will develop in order that he may encourage and accelerate the process. If we call the ideal team state the COOPERATION stage, how would we characterize the two stages through which the team has to pass before it reaches that, if it ever does?

The first stage is called the INCLUSION stage, for it is here that people determine if they are, and if they feel they are, a team member. Anxiety and introversion are common, but they may be disguised by compensatory opposite behavior in some people. The need for acceptance and the fear of rejection are strong. Perhaps your parents moved house when you were a child and you suddenly found yourself plunged into a new school of strangers in mid-term. You will recall the feelings well: the feeling of separateness and the need, the desperation to find a friend, just one friend, to feel included, to be like the others and to be liked. Group members may not be very mentally productive in this phase, for their focus will be on their emotional needs and concerns.

If there is a designated group leader the members will look to him for acceptance and guidance. They want to conform; they seek to comply. The tone and the example that the leader sets at this stage is important because it will quickly become the accepted norm of the group. For example, if the leader displays openness and honesty and discloses feelings or even a weakness of his own, others will tend to follow suit and a good relating practice will be established. It is a time of tentativeness, and a good leader will attempt to address and satisfy individual concerns so that the group as a whole can move forward. Fortunately, for many people this phase does not last too long, but for a few it may take weeks or months to feel part of the team. Those who had a childhood in which they developed a strong sense of personal security – and those who rise to leadership positions tend to be this type – would do well to be tolerant and supportive of those who were not so lucky.

Once the majority of the group feels included, another dynamic emerges, that of individual ASSERTION. It is a time of expressing power and of extending boundaries. Animals do it; they mark out their territory (the males, of course) and woe betide any opponent who dares to enter. It is the phase in which the pecking order gets worked out. The polite business term for it is the establishment of roles and functions, but the words are often nicer than the actions. Competition within the team is hot, which may even lead to exceptional individual performances, sometimes at the expense of others. It is a phase in which people try out and discover their strengths, and the team may make up in productivity what it lacks in cohesiveness.

This is an important and valuable development phase, but it can be tough for the leader. There will be challenges to the leadership. Team members have to find out that they can disagree with the leader before they will be willing to agree. They need to exercise their will internally, in order to hone it for team application externally. A good group leader will offer, and encourage team members to take, responsibilities and thereby satisfy their assertion needs. It is important that the leader allows the challenges, but unfortunately many leaders are threatened by them, and hunker down and assert their own authority in order to control the process. It requires a balancing act.

Those who run training groups often experience this phase of a five-day training group as the 'kill the trainer' day. It generally begins toward the evening of the second day, but a good leader usually manages to be 'resurrected again' during the third day. If this phase coincides with the visit of an outside presenter, he may be given a very rough ride for little apparent reason! This is all a necessary, even healthy, part of group dynamics, but all too often, particularly among the reserved British, the interplays remain covert for the sake of appearances and they therefore take longer to work themselves out.

As I have said, a team in this phase can be quite productive, which may shield the recognition of yet greater potential. In fact, the majority of business or sports teams seldom advance beyond this phase, by and large because that is about as far as our whole western industrial society has collectively reached. To go beyond this is therefore to go above the norm, but that is not as difficult to achieve as is generally thought – with coaching.

At the beginning of this chapter we examined some of the most positive characteristics prevalent in the COOPERATION phase of a team. I do not wish to imply that such a team would be all sweetness and light. In fact, a danger of the COOPERATION stage is that an overemphasis on the group develops, which becomes too comfortable and which does not allow for any dissent. The most productive teams will be highly cooperative but will retain a degree of dynamic tension. The best team leaders preserve this sensitively.

COOPERATION

Team development stage	Characteristics		Maslow's hierarchy of needs
COOPERATION (performing)	Interdependent	Energy directed outward to common goals	Self-actualizing
(norming)			
ASSERTION (storming)	Independent	Energy focused on internal competition	Self-esteem Esteem from others
INCLUSION (forming)	Dependent	Energy turned inward within team members	Belonging

The above table shows, in parentheses, another set of labels for the same team-developmental sequence, and also some of the main distinguishing team characteristics. There are more.

For example, if a team is in the COOPERATION stage and one of its members has a bad day, the others will rally round and support. If it is in the ASSERTION stage, the others may quietly celebrate the fall of a competitor. If it is in the INCLUSION stage, few will know or care.

On the other hand, if a team is in the COOPERATION stage and a team member has a personal triumph, the rest will join in celebration. However, if the team is in the ASSERTION stage, the rest may become jealous. If the team is in the INCLUSION stage, the others could even feel threatened.

Maslow's hierarchy of needs   We have looked extensively at Maslow's model in the chapter on motivation, and the top three needs in individual development terms run parallel to this team development model. A team of self-actualizing individuals, if they could be found, would quickly attain the dizzy heights of COOPERATION and outstanding results. A team of those seeking self-esteem would perform very well individually but would be inclined to 'do their own thing'. People seeking the esteem of others would compete strongly against each other, producing some great performances – and some losers. A team of individuals seeking to belong would be compliant and irritatingly helpful, more in words than deeds.

Of course, the divisions between these three stages are permeable and overlapping, and the position and state of the team are subject to fluctuation when there is any turnover in team personnel.

MACROCOSM

Nevertheless, few readers will fail to recognize these stages and their characteristics from their own experience at work or at play. One macrocosmic example to challenge your mind is the suggestion that the whole of western industrial society is in the latter days of the ASSERTION stage with a few early signs of COOPERATION showing through (concern for the environment; the development of European integration). The collapse of the Soviet empire was the inevitable result of the attempt to coerce that society into the COOPERATION stage without allowing organic development through the previous stages. And the attempts to redraw the map in eastern Europe and elsewhere are a manifestation of a temporary backslide into INCLUSION issues. For some, even SURVIVAL and SAFETY are foreground.

So if we can accept the idea that development of this general nature is common among teams of all shapes and sizes, it follows that we can resist and thereby retard team development, or we can encourage and accelerate it.

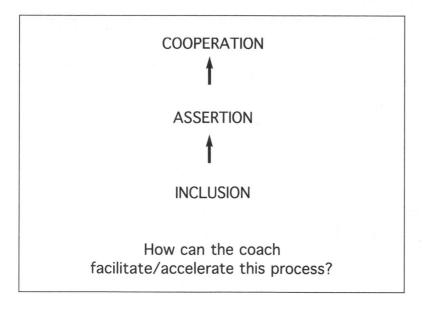

It could be said that at the start of the twenty-first century it is even more difficult to get the best out of a team. The reasons for this include the following:

TEAMS TODAY

❏ People no longer work in settled groupings but are continually forming and re-forming teams.
❏ Some teams are spread across geographic boundaries, making contact more infrequent and more problematic.
❏ The time scales within which teams are expected to join, form and perform to meet a business challenge are shorter than ever before.
❏ The business challenges themselves have increased in complexity.
❏ Not all groups of people who collaborate need to be in a team to achieve their objectives.

The result is that coaching has a very important role to play in helping people to work well together. For example, it can help people establish whether and when they need to be in a team. Both groups and teams are valid ways of working and coaching applies to both. How it is best used with teams is addressed in the following chapter.

19
Coaching Teams

*I*t is said that a manager only has two functions: first to get the job done and second to develop his people. As we have said before, all too often managers are too busy doing the first to get around to the second. However, both functions are combined when coaching is used as the management style. So it is in teams – when the team is managed by coaching the job gets done well and the team develops at the same time. We will look here, however, at different applications of team coaching for task performance and for team development.

TASK PERFORMANCE

The coaching of a team to perform a task is based on the same principles as coaching individuals. The more aware a team is both individually and collectively, the better it will perform.

Imagine that a business team is tackling a new task. The team leader may coach its members together by asking them questions. If it is a large group or team, the leader might ask rhetorical questions and get the team members in pairs or trios to discuss their responses with each other and then report on their conclusions to the whole group. He might mix people with different functions for this process to stimulate new ideas. He might himself participate in one of the pairs or trios.

By this method the team members would formulate their various GOALS. They would all provide the necessary input to the clear understanding of the REALITY. The resources and ideas of the whole team are employed to brainstorm the OPTIONS and an agreed action plan is reached and driven forward by the combined WILL of the group. Of course, the team leader not only asks the coaching questions but gives his own input at any time. Such a process does take a little longer than a prescriptive team briefing, but the performance of the task will be incomparably better if all resources are pooled and the whole team becomes aware and responsible.

In some situations the team leader will group coach, for example in reviewing the team's past performance of a task. He may do this with all team members responding to his questions, but he might also ask them to write rather than speak their responses. This enables each of them at the same time to examine in detail their individual contribution to the overall task.

The questions might run as follows:

❏ What was the most difficult/time-consuming/stressful part of the task for you?
❏ How long did it take?
❏ What was difficult about it?
❏ What would you do differently next time?
❏ Who needs to know about the changes you will make?
❏ What support do you need? From whom? How will you get it?
❏ If you did that, how might it affect the result/the others/the quality/the time?

Each team member can then briefly share with the others what they came up with and resolve any conflicting changes. This process is very thorough, it brings out detail, it ensures clarity and understanding, it draws on all the team's resources, it promotes ownership and commitment and it builds self-esteem and self-motivation.

To some team managers all this may sound unnecessary at best, and a load of rubbish at worst. Some will continue to believe that participation, involvement, self-esteem, shared responsibility, satisfaction and quality of life in the workplace are luxuries we can ill afford and that they contribute nothing to performance. The arguments given here will not of themselves convince them otherwise, but in time their dwindling, disaffected workforce and their inability to build teams may do so.

COACHING BY EXAMPLE

It is most important for a manager to establish a 'right' relationship with the team members under his charge from the moment he meets them. His behavior will be taken by the team members as the model for their behavior. They will tend to emulate him, even though initially they are likely to do so primarily as a means of gaining his approval while they are in the INCLUSION stage of team development.

If the team leader wishes to establish openness and honesty in the team, then he needs to be open and honest from the outset. If he wants the team members to trust him and each other, he must demonstrate trust and trustworthiness. If he sees the benefit in social contact outside work among the team, then he needs to participate in and perhaps initiate it himself.

Since the majority of individuals and teams still expect somewhat autocratic leadership, they might be surprised, even confused, by a leader who begins on a very participative note. A few might even imagine him to be weak or unsure of himself. It is advisable for him to preempt this on day one by describing his intended management style and inviting questions about it.

The manager or team leader also needs to be clear about his own willingness to invest time and energy in developing his team with a view to quality long-term relationships and performance, as opposed to merely getting the job done in the short term. If the manager only pays lip service to team-building principles, he will get no more than he pays for. Dedication to team process pays off.

Coaching is the primary tool for both managing and developing teams. Peter Lenney, a general manager in Courtaulds Coatings, told *Management Today* (December, 1991) that 'if you can't coach, you can't manage' became something of a corporate axiom. I agree wholeheartedly. David Kenney, Management Development Manager of Boots the Chemist, says that part of his mission is 'to ensure that 100 percent of our managers behave as good coaches'.

THE APPLICATION OF COACHING IN TEAMS

The team development model described in the previous chapter forms an excellent basis for the application of coaching in teams. If the manager or coach understands that teams perform at their best when they reach the COOPERATION stage, he will use coaching with the team as a whole and with individual members to generate upward progress through the stages. For example, if the agreed GOAL is to lift the team into the COOPERATION stage and the REALITY is that it is now somewhere between the INCLUSION and the ASSERTION stages, what OPTIONS do we have and what WILL we do?

The list of OPTIONS that follows has been compiled from the responses to that question given by participants in the team-building programs that I run.

OPTIONS TO ACHIEVE TEAM COOPERATION

Discuss and agree the definition of a set of common goals for the team This should be done within the team regardless of whether the organization has defined the team's goal. There is always room for modification and for deciding how it should be done. Each team member should be invited to contribute and also to add any personal goals that might be embraced within the overall team goal.

Develop a set of ground rules or operating principles acceptable to all team members and to which all have contributed All should agree to abide by these even if they are not wholeheartedly behind every one of them. If they want to have their wishes included, it is essential that they agree to respect those of others. These ground rules should be subject to regular checking as to whether they are being adhered to and whether they need to be changed or updated. If all parties agree these rules in sincerity and have good intentions, harsh recriminations should not be made for lapses unless they become frequent.

Many of the suggestions that follow could be included as ground rules, but I will continue to list them separately.

Set aside time on a regular basis, usually in conjunction with a scheduled task meeting, for group process work During this time ground rules are reviewed, appreciations and gripes are expressed and personal sharing might be included so that openness and trust are built, and also so that team members are acknowledged as people, not just as cogs in a production machine. This period should not be allowed to be taken over by task talk.

Canvass team members' views about the desirability of arranging structured social time together If a regular event is planned, the preference of an individual not to attend because of prior commitments or the need for more family time must be respected. He, on the other hand, needs to be prepared for some feeling of separateness as a consequence of his choice.

Put support systems in place to deal, in confidence if requested, with individual troubles or concerns as they arise If process meetings cannot be held frequently for geographic or other reasons, a buddy system might be instituted whereby each member of the team has another member as a buddy to whom they can talk if necessary. This way minor issues can be resolved promptly and valuable process meeting time is not wasted.

Develop a common interest outside work Some teams have found that a group activity such as a sport or a common interest outside work that is shared by all can be very binding for the team. I recall one team who 'adopted' a child in a developing country and, with a small monthly contribution each, paid for her schooling. They felt that she had contributed even more to their lives than they had to hers.

Learn a new skill together   Similar to the option above but more task oriented, some teams have agreed to learn a new skill such as coaching, or a language, or to attend a work-related course together. This might even be in healthy competition with other regional teams, for example, in the same organization.

Practice the qualities exercise together Team relationships benefit greatly from team members doing appropriate variations among themselves of the qualities exercise explained in Chapter 17. This throws light on certain qualities, thereby helping to grow them. It also builds trust, understanding and openness among team members remarkably quickly. It can be repeated in similar or different forms on a regular basis, for example at every other process meeting.

Hold group discussions on individual and collective meaning and purpose as perceived by group members This is both broader and deeper than exploring goals. Meaning and purpose are what drive people, and a lack of them leads to lethargy, depression and poor health. Throwing more light or awareness on something so pervasive that we are barely conscious of it will increase purposefulness and the quality of life at work and at home.

Each of these suggestions or OPTIONS can be considered by the team using a coaching approach. That is to say that they may be introduced or quietly facilitated by the team leader, but should be decided on by the team members themselves. The decision to adopt one or more of them must be made democratically, but it also must be specific and recorded in ways recommended in Chapter 10 on WILL. Remember that the basis of coaching to improve team performance is not imposing but increasing individual and collective AWARENESS and RESPONSIBILITY.

20
Overcoming Barriers to Coaching

We have looked at the context of coaching, its value and its irrefutable logic. There is no mystique about coaching. It is not difficult to learn. However, it cannot be learned from a book, any more than driving a car or a golf ball can. Like all skills, it requires practice. If that practice is undertaken with commitment, and with AWARENESS and RESPONSIBILITY, it does not take long to become proficient and relaxed in its use, and to benefit from its results.

A NEW VISION OF PEOPLE

For some people, coaching both demands and causes a fundamental change in the way they perceive themselves and others, be they colleagues, subordinates or competitors. To see all people as having the potential to be great in their chosen field, just as an acorn has, is a far cry from the more common but outmoded perception of people as empty vessels of little worth until given outside input. That shift may take time or it may come as a revelation, but even before it takes place, and while the underlying philosophy still seems foreign, it is possible to raise performance levels quite effectively by simply following the principles of good coaching prescribed in this book.

Nothing is plain sailing, however, and you are liable to meet a few barriers along the way. Perhaps the greatest barrier is difficult people, which expressed as a concern is: 'How do I coach difficult people?' This is very often raised, but more in fear and anticipation than from any actual negative experiences. If coaching is introduced sensitively, it is often accepted with no difficulty or, better still, welcomed. That is not to say that everyone readily accepts coaching, nevertheless. Any change of behavior by a manager is viewed with suspicion by some and may be met with a level of resistance.

I have suggested before that it is easier to learn the new – the basics of coaching – than it is to give up the old – telling. We are conditioned by a long history of telling and being told. The expectation and therefore the wish to be told are ingrained in us, even if there are benefits to being asked. It is no bad thing to explain to and remind those we manage or coach what the benefits to them personally are: learning to think for themselves, greater awareness in all things that enhances performance, learning and enjoyment, more choice, greater sense of responsibility, enhanced self-belief, possible promotion, learning to self-coach and to coach others in and out of the workplace. The benefits are legion but there may still be resistance. What are they resisting? Change in the first instance, questions secondly.

When we were asked questions by our parents, it was often because we had done something wrong. For example 'Why did you do that?', for which there was no safe answer; we were in trouble anyway. When we were asked questions by our schoolteachers, it was to test either our knowledge or whether we had been paying attention. In each case it was important to get the answer right, so questions themselves came to be seen as a threat.

It is not surprising, therefore, that to some people coaching questions are intimidating too, and so the coach must put them at their ease, build trust and be non-judgmental about their responses. It may also help simply to explain and demonstrate that the purpose of coaching questions is to raise awareness, not to test. There are seldom 'right' answers to coaching questions, just honest ones.

If resistance persists, coachees are either resisting being more aware or being more responsible, probably because they feel that these will take them out of their comfort zone. They may be afraid that questions will cause them to reveal to themselves or others the ghosts that they fear lurk within their psyche. Childhood conditioning may have taught them never to show their emotions or any other human weakness lest someone should take advantage of them. However irritating their paranoia may be, a patient and compassionate approach is likely to be the best way forward.

Of course, there are some people who are difficult about most things. This may stem from deep hostility toward the company or the manager, or toward people in general for some reason. The more likely scenario is simply a reluctant employee who wants to do enough to get by and no more: 'That is all I'm paid for. Don't ask me to think things out for myself. You're the manager, you're paid to do that.'

This is hard to change, but the key is the fact that people with such an attitude can't enjoy their working lives. A 'softly, softly' approach that helps them to discover that their quality of life in the workplace may improve if they cooperate with coaching is probably the only way. Bring coaching questions in so gradually that the person doesn't even know he is beng coached; in fact they are not at this stage, you are merely asking them questions a little more frequently than you did before.

The barriers below are drawn from lists created by participants during our coaching programs. They are all expressed here as if they are real rather than assumed and constructed by the manager or potential coach. Of course, if they are perceived as real they are effectively real until they can be recognized as a *personal concern within which lies some truth*.

I have listed the barriers in external and internal categories, in the way course participants tend to divide them. I will make a few comments on each and repeat some mentioned above to show how they are usually categorized.

The company culture is against this kind of approach Of course it is, to some extent, or you would not only now be introducing coaching. A coaching philosophy is part of the new company culture that the enlightened people in your organization are trying to create. Others prefer the boring illusion of the security of the status quo. However, more and more organizations are coming to the conclusion that survival in future may depend on change now, and that the status quo is actually the riskier alternative.

People are cynical of any new approach Yes, some of them probably will be, especially if communication within your organization has not been the best. It is important to tell them what you will do differently, and why.

They won't understand what I'm doing and won't trust me Same as the one above.

They'll know I've been on a course and give me a few weeks to get back to 'normal' Same as the one above.

They'll think it's just a new management gimmick Explain that it is not a gimmick but a necessity for improved performance and for better staff relations. They will soon discover that it is no gimmick, unless that is how you yourself see it.

It takes too long – I would rarely have the time to coach It all depends when you start and when you stop the timer. In the moment it is usually quicker to tell people what to do, but if they immediately forget and you have to tell them again … and again … and again, or if you have to keep looking over their shoulder, which takes longer?

Let me quote a user of coaching, Cameron Burness, a production-plant manager with ICI Pharmaceuticals:

Everything I do is essentially performance-aimed. I use coaching as a means of getting my staff to a level where I can delegate work to them which I would otherwise have to do myself. I see the time I spend coaching very much as an investment, the dividend from which is the far greater time I save myself through delegation.

If there is a fire, I won't hesitate to yell 'Get out of here!' – but unless I actively seek opportunities to GROW my staff by coaching them, I will be stuck in the fire-fighting cycle.

They expect to be told If they have always been told in the past, then they will expect to be told. That is not the same thing as preferring to be told.

They want to be told – they don't want responsibility If people have never been given responsibility by their parents, at school, or at work, it will seem scary at first, like anything new. Underneath, the majority of us crave responsibility, in part because it provides us with a measure of self-worth. Those with very low self-worth have a hard time with responsibility. It is another cycle to get stuck in, but coaching is the best way I know to help people out of it. A few of the relevant coaching questions might be:

❏ What do you want from work apart from money?
❏ What does responsibility mean to you?
❏ Do you feel a burden of responsibility right now?
❏ Is responsibility always a burden to you?
❏ What do you think some people like about responsibility?
❏ What else are you responsible for in your life?
❏ What are you afraid of?
❏ What could you do to overcome that?
❏ What are you willing to take responsibility for?
❏ Are you willing to try accepting more responsibility for a week?

Merely by answering these questions, they are beginning to take on responsibility – at least for their own answers and choices. If you, as their manager, won't help them to take responsibility, who will? And are you satisfied with the minimal performance that an irresponsible person provides?

They'll think I've gone nuts They may! So what? Madness is so endearing! Just explain.

I'll lose my authority   A manager who manages by coaching gains real respect, as well as self-respect, which is far more gratifying than the illusion of power that props up autocrats until they fade or fall.

I'm an expert and they respect and expect my knowledgeable input   Your expertise will still be invaluable; only the way you use it will change. Do you begrudge others acquiring some of it from you? Do you dispense your knowledge in small bites, so no one can get enough of it to threaten you? Or do you want to encourage your would-be successors to stand on your shoulders?

I already use a coaching style – I don't need to change anything   One of the classic ways of avoiding having to change is to claim that you already do it. Such people usually have a very poor version of coaching buried somewhere in the bottom of their managerial kitbag. To find out if they use it, ask their subordinates. But be careful, this may also be one of your own internal barriers. Is it? See below.

INTERNAL BARRIERS

It's nothing new – I've done it for years   If this is your arrogant response, then for certain you haven't!

I'm afraid I won't do it well   Without practice you won't. Self-coaching is the least risky place to start. Try it out with the five-a-side football team or with your son or daughter. At work there will be some individuals and teams who are easier to work with than others. Try it out with them, and tell them what you are doing.

I'll get stuck – I won't know what question to ask   This won't happen if you follow the golden rule of listening to and watching the coachee, and following their interest, lead or direction. They will always indicate what you should ask. Remember you are an awareness raiser, not an instructor. Keep it simple; the whole process is simply variations on the following theme:

What do you want?	GOAL
What is happening?	REALITY
What could you do?	OPTIONS
What will you do?	WILL

I won't get the results I get with my old style   No, you won't. You will soon get better ones!

What I did before worked, why change?   Because the survival of your organization and yourself may be dependent on better performance and better quality of life in the workplace.

I don't believe in these new softly, softly approaches   Too bad, but have you ever tried using one?

The only thing that motivates people is money   Ample recent research shows that that is not true, but it may appear to be until you learn how to offer them something more meaningful – see Chapter 13.

Most perceived external obstacles have a major internal component

MORE INTERNAL BARRIERS

Now add your own list of external barriers to this section, but simply precede each one with the phrase 'The belief I hold that...' I do not suggest that your external barriers have no validity out there, but you would do well to acknowledge that a goodly portion of them are internal ones.

We all prefer to believe that *they* are the problem; it makes us right and saves us having to change. But it also means we are stuck with the situation because we can't change *them*. If we can admit that it may be our own resistance that we project on to *them*, we are empowered to change things, because they are now under our control!

This is just another instance of self-AWARENESS and of taking RESPONSIBILITY leading to improved managerial performance.

LETTING GO

No matter how much better the new might be, letting go of the old symbols of our security is always hard. But learning and adopting new behaviors demands that we let go of old ones. The system and skill of coaching are simple and not hard to learn. Letting go of a well-used command-and-control habit to make room for coaching is much harder. I find it is often more productive to allocate time and focus to provoking and assisting people to let go of the old rather than to teaching the new. Once they do let go of the old, the new rushes in to fill the vacuum. Remove the blocks and the potential emerges.

Coaching is, after all, a natural skill and one that perhaps does not have to be taught at all if the opening is there. Loving parents who have never learned to coach use it very effectively with their children for everything from tying shoelaces to doing maths homework. They use it with their children because they care for them and about their learning and growth. If managers cared a little more for their staff, they would use coaching naturally too. If executives cared a little more for their managers than for their bottom line, even they might coach – and the bottom line would take care of itself.

So often it is when we let go of the need fo control that we gain control

21
The Multiple Benefits of Coaching

So what, then, are the benefits of coaching as opposed to instructing to the manager and the managed, and what are the benefits to an organization of adopting what I call a coaching culture?

IMPROVED PERFORMANCE AND PRODUCTIVITY

This must be number one, and we would not do it if it did not work. Coaching brings out the best in individuals and in teams, something that instructing does not even aspire to do, so how could it?

STAFF DEVELOPMENT

As I have stated earlier, developing people does not mean just sending them on a short course once or twice a year. The way you manage will either develop them or hold them back. It's up to you.

IMPROVED LEARNING

Coaching is learning on the fast track, without loss of time from the bench or desk. Enjoyment and retention are also enhanced.

IMPROVED RELATIONSHIPS

The very act of asking someone a question values them and their answer. If I only tell, there is no exchange. I might as well be talking to a load of bricks. I once asked a particularly silent but promising junior tennis player what he thought was good about his forehand. He smiled and said, 'I don't know. Nobody has ever asked me my opinion before.' That said it all to me.

Out of the respect for individuals, the improved relationships and the success that will accompany coaching, the atmosphere at work will change for the better.

IMPROVED QUALITY OF LIFE FOR INDIVIDUALS

Staff who are coached, who welcome responsibility, do not have to be chased or watched, freeing the manager to perform his more overarching functions, which in the past he never found the time to do well.

MORE TIME FOR THE MANAGER

Coaching and a coaching environment encourage creative suggestions from all members of a team without the fear of ridicule or premature dismissal. One creative idea often sparks off others.

MORE CREATIVE IDEAS

A manager very often has no idea what hidden resources are available to him until he starts coaching. He will soon uncover many previously undeclared talents in his team as well as solutions to practical problems, which can only be found by those who have to carry out a task regularly.

BETTER USE OF PEOPLE, SKILLS AND RESOURCES

In an atmosphere in which people are valued, they are invariably willing to push the boat out when or even before being called on to do so. In far too many organizations, where people are not valued, they only do what they are told, and as little as possible at that.

FASTER AND MORE EFFECTIVE EMERGENCY RESPONSE

The coaching ethos is all about change, being responsive and responsible. In future the demand for flexibility will increase, not decrease. Increased competition in the market, technological innovation, instant global communication, economic uncertainty and social instability will see to that throughout our brief lifetime! Only the flexible and resilient will survive.

GREATER FLEXIBILITY AND ADAPTABILITY TO CHANGE

MORE MOTIVATED STAFF

I repeat here that both the carrot and the stick have lost their edge and that people perform because they want to, not because they have to. Coaching helps people to discover their self-motivation.

CULTURE CHANGE

The coaching principles underpin the management style of the high-performance culture to which so many business leaders aspire. Any coaching program will help make culture transformation more realizable.

A LIFE SKILL

Coaching is both an attitude and a behavior, with multiple applications both in and out of work. It is more and more in demand, so even those who are looking to change their job soon are going to find it an invaluable skill wherever they go.

COACHING TO WIN

Let me return to sport, at least to a unique and hazardous competitive event. It was renowned for its tradition of autocratic leadership, which has produced remarkable performances in the past, but which was diametrically opposed to the coaching philosophy.

Every year the highlight of that great military show that used to be held each summer in London, the Royal Tournament, was the Field Gun race. Initiated many years ago to commemorate a heroic campaign in the Boer War in which artillery was manhandled over mountains, the event consisted of a race to partially dismantle and drag an ancient gun carriage over an obstacle course that would be daunting enough to most of us without the baggage. The contestants were three branches of the British navy.

Each year they were only allowed nine weeks to assemble and train their sixteen-man teams. In 1990, Joe Gough was the first trainer for the Fleet Air Arm team. Before training started, he attended a two-day Performance Coaching course run by my colleague David Hemery and myself, and subsequently David visited the team in Southampton early in their training run-up. As a result, Joe courageously and radically altered his approach. After the event Joe said, 'We changed everything this year, and if we'd failed I'd have been pilloried, but right now I'm the most popular man in the Fleet Air Arm!'

For the first time in the history of the event one service won all five major trophies. The Fleet Air Arm 'A' team recorded the fastest time, the best aggregate time, the most points and the fewest penalties, and the 'B' team also won its trophy. This outstanding result was achieved with 30 percent fewer practice runs than in previous years and with fewer injuries.

Here are some quotes from the team:

❏ 'This was the first time that someone had asked our opinion and listened.'
❏ 'Joe would ask us if we wanted to do another run, and if we said no, we felt we owed him a bit, and that was a positive carry over to the next day.'
❏ 'Joe was very approachable. He treated us like men.'
❏ 'One night Joe told us to rig up for another run, and we were shattered. Eric, our PTI, went and told Joe that he and the team thought his decision was wrong. Joe came out and told us to stow it away! I couldn't believe it. It takes a big man to admit he was wrong … and once he had done that, the rest of us started admitting that we had been wrong on parts of our drill practices, instead of making excuses. There was a lot more honesty all round.'

Joe Gough summed up his new-found conviction that coaching really does produce better performances than commanding and fear can, when he said: 'You can **make** a man run, but you can't **make** him run fast!'

For me the benefits of coaching far outweigh the barriers. Do they for you?

22
Conclusion

Coaching is a nicer way to do better business.

This is a short book about coaching; if it had been any longer you might not have purchased it, or might not have read this far. I may have included some things that you did not need, I may have left out other things that you might have liked. It may have been too shallow in parts, or too deep in others.

It was my intention to persuade you that coaching is a skill that all people who teach or manage others would do well to acquire. The need for better people skills is growing and will continue to do so in the foreseeable future in business, in the service industries, in our schools and in sport.

Coaching is, as you have now seen, infinitely more than a tool that managers can use in a variety of situations such as planning, delegation or problem solving. It is a different way of viewing people, a far more optimistic way than most of us are accustomed to, and it results in a different way of treating them. It requires us to suspend limiting beliefs about people, including ourselves, abandon old habits and liberate ourselves from redundant ways of thinking.

As with any new skill, attitude, style or belief, adopting a coaching ethos will require commitment, practice and some time before it flows naturally and its effectiveness is optimized. Some will find it easier than others. If coaching is already your style, I hope this book will help you take what you already do to greater heights, or provide you with a fuller rationale for what you already do intuitively. If it has not been your style in the past, I hope the book will help set you on some new ways of thinking about management, about performance and about people. It will also provide you with some coaching guidelines within which to begin your practice.

PRACTICE

There is no one right way to coach. This book is no more than a map to help you decide where you want to go, and to introduce you to some routes toward your goal. You will have to explore the territory for yourself, since no map can portray the infinite variety in the landscape of human interplay. The richness of that landscape can turn people management into a personal and unique art form with which to decorate, appreciate and enjoy your place of work.

NO ONE RIGHT WAY

I remain steadfastly optimistic about the future of coaching. It is undeniable that coaching, or the principles on which it is based, is becoming ever more widely recognized and used. We may drop the word coaching or add new terms to the crop that already exist: counseling, facilitating, empowering, mentoring, supporting, guiding, psychotherapy. Their applications differ somewhat but they overlap, and though they may be expressed differently, the underlying principles of awareness, responsibility and self-belief are common to all. These principles are at the very core of human growth and effectiveness.

CAUSE FOR OPTIMISM

My optimism is rooted in the positive yearning of the indomitable human spirit. As hinted at in Chapters 14–16, I believe that business is somewhat off track, through not yet off the rails. It feeds off and appeals to our lower nature, power and greed, but at the same time it can be a vehicle for our creativity, aspiration and the will to good. Business is the most powerful man-made organizing force on earth and along with education it is the vehicle through which transformation can most effectively come about, driven by the human spirit. But business urgently needs to get back on track and align itself with higher and more caring human values.

To facilitate that alignment, the best people skills are going to be at a premium. Coaching is one of the most business-friendly skills for human growth. I hope this book continues to foster the development of coaching and that the additions in this third edition will supplement what has appeared before. If these musings seem fanciful, misguided or just plain mad to the pragmatist in you, I hope at least we may all agree that *coaching is a nicer way to do better business.*

Appendix

Performance coaching is based on:

CONTEXT   Awareness and Responsibility

SKILLS   Effective questioning
               Active listening

SEQUENCE   G – Goals: What do you want?
           R – Reality: What is happening now?
           O – Options: What could you do?
           W – Will: What will you do?

The figure overleaf illustrates the many-pronged, many-faceted nature of the benefits that all spread out from the very simple but very powerful concept of AWARENESS and RESPONSIBILITY. Following any line of arrows from top to bottom illustrates the sequence of effects.

On the following three pages is a skeleton set of coaching questions, to be elaborated on and used as a guide to a coaching session.

MANAGEMENT BY COACHING
generates

Awareness
QUALITY & QUANTITY
of INPUT

Responsibility
PERSONAL CHOICE
& CONTROL

Q&Q of output — Recall — Interest — Uniqueness — Self-esteem — Ownership

Enjoyment — Potential

Learning — Confidence

Performance — Self-motivation

**Higher productivity
Improved communication
Better working relationships
Quality of life in the workplace
Greater recognition
More customer care**

GOAL

❏ What is the subject matter or the issue on which you would like to work?

❏ What form of outcome are you seeking by the end of this coaching session?

❏ How far and how detailed do you expect to get in this session?

❏ In the long term what is your goal related to this issue? What is the time frame?

❏ What intermediate steps can you identify, with their time frames?

REALITY

❑ What is the present situation in more detail?

❑ What and how great is your concern about it?

❑ Who is affected by this issue other than you?

❑ Who knows about your desire to do something about it?

❑ How much control do you personally have over the outcome?

❑ Who else has some control over it and how much?

❑ What action steps have you taken on it so far?

❑ What stopped you from doing more?

❑ What obstacles will need to be overcome on the way?

❑ What, if any, internal obstacles or personal resistances do you have to taking action?

❑ What resources do you already have? Skill, time, enthusiasm, money, support, etc.?

❑ What other resources will you need? Where will you get them from?

❑ What is really the issue here, the nub of the issue or the bottom line?

OPTIONS

❑ What are all the different ways in which you could approach this issue?

❑ Make a list of all the alternatives, large or small, complete and partial solutions.

❑ What else could you do?

❑ What would you do if you had more time, a larger budget or if you were the boss?

❑ What would you do if you could start again with a clean sheet, with a new team?

❑ Would you like to add a suggestion from me?

❑ What are the advantages and disadvantages of each of these in turn?

❏ Which would give the best result?

❏ Which of these solutions appeals to you most, or feels best to you?

❏ Which would give you the most satisfaction?

WILL

❏ Which option or options do you choose?

❏ To what extent does this meet all your objectives?

❏ What are your criteria and measurements for success?

❏ When precisely are you going to start and finish each action step?

❏ What could arise to hinder you in taking these steps or meeting the goal?

❏ What personal resistance do you have, if any, to taking these steps?

❏ What will you do to eliminate these external and internal factors?

❏ Who needs to know what your plans are?

❏ What support do you need and from whom?

❏ What will you do to obtain that support and when?

❏ What could I do to support you?

❏ What commitment on a one-to-ten scale do you have to taking these agreed actions?

❏ What prevents this from being a ten?

❏ What could you do or alter to raise your commitment closer to ten?

❏ Is there anything else you want to talk about now or are we finished?

Some solutions to the nine dot exercise

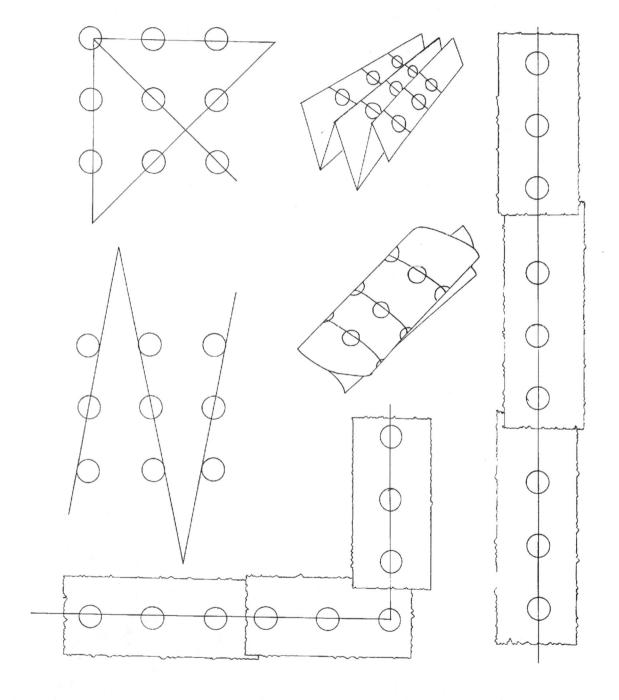

Bibliography

Barrett, Richard (1998) *Liberating the Corporate Soul*,
    Butterworth-Heinemann.

Board, Robert de (1987) *Counselling Skills*, Gower.

Clutterbuck, David (2001) *Everyone Needs a Mentor*, CIPD.

Denton, Elizabeth A (1999) A *Spiritual Audit of Corporate
    America*: A *Hard Look at Spirituality, Religion, and Values in the
    Workplace*, Jossey-Bass.

Gallwey, Timothy (1986) *The Inner Game of Tennis*, Pan.

Gallwey, Timothy (1986) *The Inner Game of Golf*, Pan.

Gallwey, Timothy (2000) *The Inner Game of Work*, Texere.

Goleman, Daniel (1996) *Emotional Intelligence*, Bloomsbury.

Goleman, Daniel (1999) *Working with Emotional Intelligence*,
    Bloomsbury.

Hawken, Paul, Lovins, Amory B. & Lovins, Hunter (2000)
    Natural Capitalism, Earthscan.

Hemery, David (1991) *Sporting Excellence*: *What Makes a
    Champion?*, Collins Willow.

Knight, Sue (2002) NLP *at Work*, Nicholas Brealey
    Publishing.

Landsberg, Max (1997) *The Tao of Coaching*, HarperCollins
    Business.

Parsloe, Eric (1992) *Coaching, Mentoring and Assessing*: A *Practical Guide to Developing Confidence*, Kogan Page.

Pilger, John (1998) *Hidden Agendas*, Vintage.

Roddick, Anita (2001) *Business as Unusual: The Triumph of Anita Roddick*, Thorsons.

Semler, Ricardo (2001) *Maverick!*, Random House Business Books.

Smith, Simon (2000) *Inner Leadership*, Nicholas Brealey Publishing.

Stayer, Ralph (1990) 'How I learned to let my workers lead', *Harvard Business Review*, November/December.

Whitmore, Diana (1999) *Psychosynthesis Counselling in Action*, Sage.

Whitworth, Laura, House, Henry & Sandahl, Philip (1998) *Co-Active Coaching*, Davies-Black Publishing.

Zohar, Danah & Marshall, Ian (2001) SQ: *Spiritual Intelligence, The Ultimate Intelligence*, Bloomsbury.

NLP AT WORK
THE DIFFERENCE THAT MAKES A DIFFERENCE IN BUSINESS
Second edition

SUE KNIGHT

*"Sympathetic and clear … the whole book makes NLP sound reasonable, achievable and commonsense.
If a good visual presentation, jargon-reduced descriptions and lots of examples of NLP at work in the workplace are your desire, this is a great place to start."*
NLP World

Neuro	the way you filter and process your experience through your senses
Linguistic	the way you interpret your experience through language
Programming	the way you code your language and behavior into your own personal program

Neuro Linguistic Programming is how you make sense of your world and most importantly how to make it what you want it to be. Other books will tell you what to do. The difference that makes a difference with NLP is that it gives you the *how*.

Sue Knight explains the difference that makes the difference between those who excel and those who 'get by' in the way they communicate, motivate, influence, negotiate, lead, empower and manage their own self-development.

This clear and reasonable guide cuts through the jargon of NLP and introduces the techniques that will enable you to:

* become more successful in any area of your life and business that you choose
* choose how you influence the people and situations around you
* improve your ability to learn new ideas
* learn how to generate 100% commitment from yourself and others
* manage your emotions so that you can be creative, constructive, influential and understanding
* be sensitive to yourself and others and communicate in a way that others will find compelling and understandable
* tap into your subconscious mind and draw on its superior processing power

With a completely revised and updated toolkit of exercises, examples and action tips this new edition of *NLP at Work* is essential reading for everyone concerned with accelerating their learning and enhancing their creativity, communication influence and impact

Sue Knight is a leading trainer and speaker on NLP for business. She pioneers the special use of NLP to improve the quality of the business world.

UK £14.99, US $19.95
Paperback 1 85788 302 0
390pp 234×189mm

LEADING YOUR TEAM
HOW TO INVOLVE AND INSPIRE TEAMS
Second edition

ANDREW LEIGH & MICHAEL MAYNARD

*"Well written, jargon-free and packed with knowledgeable advice,
this is a primer for every new manager."*
Director

At last, a readable and up-to-date guide for team leaders everywhere on the practical aspects and people skills of positive teamworking, with a wealth of ideas, tips, quotes, checklists and examples.

Leading Your Team is an invaluable resource for anyone who wants to understand how to inspire their team, how to harness the power and commitment of everyone involved, and above all how to be adaptable to changing circumstances. The authors explain through real-life examples and detailed advice what it takes to be a facilitating, supportive leader – how to ask for the moon and get it!

Right from the start the book adopts a hands-on approach. It begins with a survival kit for all leaders facing the challenge of a new or 'difficult' team. It gives step-by-step guidance on how to run an inspired team meeting, how to brief teams and set goals together, how to develop your team and review their progress, and how to create self-managing teams.

The authors offer solutions to working in multicultural and virtual teams, encouraging cooperation between teams and leading creative teams. There is also a chapter giving a strategic view of teams that considers how trainers, policy makers, consultants and team members can all make the best use of teamworking.

Major additions, including a new chapter on virtual teams, bring up-to-date the authors' classic advice on how to facilitate and inspire team excellence. A new 3-stage development process shows how to successfully make the transition from being a *player* (who takes opportunities) to a *pioneer* (who seeks opportunities) to a team *creator* (who makes opportunities).

Andrew Leigh is a Fellow of the IPD and is also the author of *20 Ways to Manage Better* and, with Michael Maynard, *The Perfect Presentation* and *Ace Teams*. **Michael Maynard** provides consultancy and training to many major corporations in the areas of personal expression, teams and personal effectiveness. Andrew Leigh and Michael Maynard are senior partners in **Maynard Leigh Associates**, a consultancy active at the cutting edge of training and development.

UK £12.99, US $19.95
Paperback 1 85788 304 7
264pp 234×189mm

MANAGING TRANSITIONS
MAKING THE MOST OF CHANGE
Second edition

WILLIAM BRIDGES

Calm, lucid and encouraging. Bridges' book remains a classic years after it first appeared - praise indeed in a time of great change. His range of anecdotes and quotations is impressive, his arguments logical and persuasive."
Management Today

"Change and rate of change are more dynamic today than ever. Bill Bridges has attacked an area of managing change that many not only avoid, but also not even recognize – the human side of change. Managing Transitions *can certainly help an organization understand change better and develop improved change strategies."*
Robert Levy, Personnel Manager, Hewlett-Packard

Everybody talks about 'managing change', but this bestseller provides both a real sense of the emotional impact of change and clear, specific guidelines for both people and organizations to successfully navigate change.

Directed at managers and employers in today's corporations, where change is necessary to revitalize and improve corporate performance, *Managing Transitions* addresses the fact that it is *people* who have to carry out the change. It not only talks about what should be done, but also shows how to do it, giving managers practical ways to bring everybody 'on board'. Armed with this new information managers will look at future changes in a new way, no longer feeling anxious and hopeless, but rather looking at the opportunities.

In this thoroughly updated and expanded second edition of the bestselling *Managing Transitions*, (over 400,000 copies sold) Bridges has added five new sections of specific advice about practical issues and a completely new chapter on the developmental 'life cycle' of an organization, illustrating how many of the most difficult changes that an organization needs to deal with come from its movement from one life-phase to the next.

William Bridges, PhD, is a consultant and lecturer based in Mill Valley, California. He is the author of the bestseller *Jobshift: How to Prosper in a Workplace Without Jobs* and its sequel *Creating You & Co*, together with the classic *Transitions* (Nicholas Brealey Publishing). Formerly a professor of English, he made a shift to the field of transition management in the mid-1970s. *The Wall Street Journal* listed him in 1993 among the ten most popular executive development consultants in the US. His several hundred clients include Shell, Pacific Bell, Intel, Apple, Procter & Gamble and Chevron.

UK only £14.99
Paperback 1 85788 341 1
181pp 234×189mm

COACHING ACROSS CULTURES
NEW TOOLS FOR LEVERAGING NATIONS, CORPORATE AND PROFESSIONAL DIFFERENCES

PHILIPPE ROSINSKI

"Coaching Across Cultures is an outstanding book that explains how to develop the new breed of leadership necessary to achieve sustainable high performance in today's global and multicultural environment. This visionary piece of work is both profound and practical. It will show you how to leverage human potential and its rich cultural diversity, to the benefit of employees, customers, shareholders and society at large."
Dean O'Hare, Chairman and Chief Executive Officer, The Chubb Corporation

Whether working across countries ot bridging corporate and professional boundaries, the demands of global business require new ways of managing and motivating people. Now there is a one-of-a-kind book that introduces a new and more creative form of coaching to meet the demands of today's diverse and international work place: *Coaching Across Cultures.*

Building on his firsthand coaching experience with executives and teams from some of the world's most respected companies - including IBM, Unilver, Chubb and Baxter Healthcare - Philippe Rosinski breaks new ground with the first book to bridge the gap between coaching and cultures.

Although the concept of culture often suggests values and behaviors of nations, *Coaching Across Cultures* expands our worldview to consider differences of every kind including corporate cultures and professional groups - from engineers and nurses to business managers. Indeed, coaching, which originated in the United States, has assumed an American worldview, a perspective that is too narrow. Culture must now become part of the equation.

The author offers both practical and effective coaching methods as well as thoughtful new approaches to help you push beyond the confines of your own cultural norms, values and beliefs when working with colleagues or coaching your clients.

Philippe Rosinski spent six years in the engineering field as a software engineer in California and as a project manager in Brussels before starting his career in coaching and leadership development. He holds a Master of Science degree in Electrical Engineering from Stanford University and the Cepac post-graduate business degree from the Solvay Business School in Brussels and is the first continental European to be designated Master Certified Coach by the International Coach Federation.

UK £19.99, US $29.95
Paperback 1 85788 301 2
337pp 231×153mm

COACHING C.L.U.E.S.
REAL STORIES, POWERFUL SOLUTIONS, PRACTICAL TOOLS

MARIAN J. THIER

"Hands-on, timely and authentic, Coaching C.L.U.E.S. *offers practical information in an engaging, personal style and fills a void as a very useful tool."*
Stacey Wilcox, Healthcare Consultant

Coaching C.L.U.E.S. delivers real stories of real people successfully mastering tough business challenges. This practical guide is packed with coaching dialogues, skill-building exercises, and 12 unique, field-tested tools - everything you need to learn how to apply the subtle power of the coaching to solve actual workplace problems and stretch your skills in delegating, brainstorming, personal organization , inquiry and advocacy, meeting management, and customer outreach.

"A virtual coach for everyone who wishes to enhance their effectiveness in working with clients, Coaching C.L.U.E.S. *offers deep wisdom from one who is herself a true master - a 'must have' addition to your library."*
Richard Whiteley, author of *The Customer Driven Company* and *The Corporate Shaman*

Framed by the five C.L.U.E.S. of coaching - **C**haracteristics, **L**anguages, **U**nderlying Motives, **E**nergy and **S**tories - *Coaching C.L.U.E.S.* presents real-world accounts of how hundreds of individuals and teams have succeeded in finding new ways to think creatively and improve their performance.

Very compelling - I found myself wanting to get to the end of the stories to see how things turned out! Coaching C.L.U.E.S. *will make a real contribution to the field with its practical and creative suggestions that OD professionals can use in their work."*
Anna Marie Valerio, Organization Leadership Consultant, IBM

Marian J. Thier, a pioneer in the field of professional coaching, is a Master Certified Coach and an international consultant. Founder and principal of Expanding Thought Inc., her worldwide Fortune 500 clients include Pfizer, Avon, Merck & Co., Occidental Petroleum, DuPont, IBM, Kaiser Permanente, Kraft, 3M and Motorola. Thier speaks and writes extensively on issues of leadership and organizational creativity through her work with the American Society for Training and Development and the International Coach Federation. She lives in Boulder, Colorado.

UK £12.99, US $19.95
Paperback 1 85788 337 3
181pp 234 x 189mm